Howard Thurman and the Quest for Community

Howard Thurman and the Quest for Community

From Prodigals to Compassionate Samaritans

David B. Gowler

Paulist Press
New York / Mahwah, NJ

Photo/Image Credits: see pages ix-x for permissions and acknowledgements.

Muriel Rukeyser, "Islands." Used by permission of William L. Rukeyser.

Howard Thurman, *With Head and Heart*, copyright © 1981, HarperCollins. Quotations used with permission.

Parts of chapters 3 and 4 are revisions of David B. Gowler, "The Enthymematic Nature of Parables: A Dialogic Reading of the Parable of the Rich Fool (Luke 12:16–20)," *Review and Expositor* 109:2 (2012): 199–217. Used with permission of *Review and Expositor* and SAGE Publications.

Initial explorations of the importance of the Prodigal Son and Good Samaritan parables in Howard Thurman's thought were published in two book chapters by David B. Gowler: "Sit and Listen; Go and Do: The Parables of the Good Samaritan and Prodigal Son in Howard Thurman's Life and Thought," 434–51, in *Anatomies of the Gospels and Beyond: Essays in Honor of R. Alan Culpepper*. E. J. Brill Biblical Interpretation Series 164. Edited by Elizabeth Struthers Malbon, Mikeal C. Parsons, and Paul N. Anderson. Leiden: E. J. Brill, 2018.
"From Prodigals to Good Samaritans: One Path to Common Ground in Howard Thurman's Thought," 50–65, in *The Unfinished Search for Common Ground: Reimagining Howard Thurman*. Edited by Walter Fluker. Maryknoll, NY: Orbis Books, 2023.

Cover image photos of Howard Thurman from the I. G. Bailey and Thurman family papers, Stuart A. Rose Manuscript, Archives, and Rare Book Library, Emory University. Used with permission of Anton H. Wong and Suzanne Mari Chiarenza.
Cover and book design by Lynn Else

Library of Congress Cataloging-in-Publication Data
Names: Gowler, David B., 1958-, author.
Title: Howard Thurman and the quest for community: from prodigals to compassionate Samaritans / David B. Gowler.
Description: New York, Mahwah, NJ: Paulist Press, [2024] | Summary: "Building on Howard Thurman's insights into the parables of the Prodigal Son and the Good Samaritan, this book demonstrates how these two parables are foundational to Christian life and practice"—Provided by publisher.
Identifiers: LCCN 2024006226 (print) | LCCN 2024006227 (ebook) | ISBN 9780809156948 (paperback) | ISBN 9780809188109 (ebook)
Subjects: LCSH: Good Samaritan (Parable) | Prodigal son (Parable) | Thurman, Howard, 1900–1981.
Classification: LCC BT378.G6 G677 2024 (print) | LCC BT378.G6 (ebook) | DDC 226.8—dc23/eng/20240604
LC record available at https://lccn.loc.gov/2024006226
LC ebook record available at https://lccn.loc.gov/2024006227

ISBN 978-0-8091-5694-8 (paperback)
ISBN 978-0-8091-8810-9 (ebook)

Published by Paulist Press
997 Macarthur Boulevard
Mahwah, NJ 07430
www.paulistpress.com

Printed and bound in the
United States of America

For Rita
Among the host of others to whom I am indebted,
by far I owe the greatest debt to you.

CONTENTS

LIST OF IMAGES

"The Live Oak." Boyhood home of Howard Thurman.
Photo courtesy of author.

PREFACE

> Eventually I discovered that the oak tree and I had a unique relationship. I could sit, with my back against its trunk, and feel the same peace that would come to me in my bed at night. I could reach down in the quiet places of my spirit, take out my bruises and my joys, unfold them, and talk about them. I could talk aloud to the oak tree and know that I was understood. It, too, was a part of my reality, like the woods, the night, and the pounding surf, my earliest companions, giving me space.
>
> Howard Thurman[1]

I sat under the old live oak tree in the backyard of Howard Thurman's boyhood home in Daytona Beach, Florida. As I leaned against its trunk, I tried to imagine Thurman himself sitting there as a boy, what it must have felt like for him as he talked to the tree, sharing his inner thoughts, frustrations, hopes, and dreams in the midst of the challenges he faced.

I also reflected on my own journey how, as a scholar with particular interest in the historical Jesus and his parables, I ended up studying Thurman's "footprints of a dream" to community.[2] Because of our differences, should we have met, in many ways Thurman and I initially would have been, echoing his words, "like strangers."[3]

What first drew me to Thurman is the fact that we share a deep interest in the life and teachings of Jesus and their ethical implications. In addition to the rigor and methods that a historian must use to research any subject or person, I also appreciate Thurman's insights about the "imagination" and "self-projection" it takes to try to understand the contexts of other human beings, working to put oneself in their place.[4] Such "imagination" is difficult and imperfect, because we can never fully know others' situations, but it is critical to creating understanding and then community: "Imagination is the creative vehicle that carries one spirit into the dwelling place of another."[5]

The footprints of my pilgrimage to write this book began many years ago when I read Thurman's *Jesus and the Disinherited*.[6] Because of my own work on the teachings of Jesus, especially his parables, I recognized how well Thurman had captured the essence of who Jesus was and what Jesus meant for those with their "backs against the wall," including the ethical imperatives for those whose backs were not against the wall. Thurman saw clearly how Jesus's religion and ethical vision are embedded in his first-century contexts as a Jew living in poverty, a member of a minority group oppressed by a dominant, controlling group, the Romans.[7]

The question Thurman strove to answer is one that has—or should have—concerned Christians for two millennia: How can one make the teachings of Jesus of Nazareth relevant for contemporary society? My research had led me to conclude that Jesus was a first-century apocalyptic prophet of Jewish restoration theology who, like many other Jewish prophets before him, proclaimed a message of social and economic justice for his oppressed people. Jesus's teachings are Torah centered and incorporate aspects of Jewish Wisdom traditions, the ethical import of which represents a "voice from below," a humane, commonsense approach of a first-century Jewish nonelite person. From my perspective, then, Thurman's *Jesus and the Disinherited* brilliantly bridges the gap from the first century CE to today.

The second major step toward the writing of this book came when Kipton Jensen, professor at Morehouse College, invited me to work with him on a project that would benefit from his expertise in Thurman—including Kipton's significant contributions about Thurman's importance as a philosopher[8]—and mine in the historical Jesus and his parables: a volume containing (mostly) unpublished sermons by Thurman on the parables of Jesus.[9] Listening to and reading Thurman's sermons for that book led me to see how the parables of the Prodigal Son and Good Samaritan are foundational to Thurman's life and thought, and in our continuing search for community, since he uses them to exemplify a path to reconciliation, restoration, and community with God and our fellow human beings.

The final step to my decision to write this book was a conversation with Luther Smith, who, among his many other accomplishments, for several decades has been one of the foremost authorities on Howard Thurman. This conversation led me to reflect again on how many New Testament interpreters have not grasped the significance of Thurman's contributions to our understanding Jesus as a member of a disinherited group and helped precipitate this book, with its focus on making scholarly interpretations of the parables of the Prodigal Son and Good Samaritan more understandable and presenting Thurman's interpretations of those parables in ways that illuminate what these parables mean, how they work, and what they want: love of God, love of neighbor, and the community with God and neighbor that results.

In addition, this book has another goal: to serve its readers as "a lighted lantern by the roadside at night to cheer the weary traveler," or as "a jar of cool water and a bit of fruit at the road's turning,"[10] because all of us are on a common quest and journey.

TWO CAVEATS

This book includes extensive quotations from Thurman's books, papers, lectures, sermons, and other materials, ranging from 1924 to 1981. The amount and nature of the materials from Thurman over those many decades lead me to offer two caveats for readers of this book.

First, after much reflection, I decided to preserve the exact words in Thurman's publications, archival materials, and the audios of his sermons that I transcribed so that readers can better approximate Thurman's spirit, insights, and the distinctive ways in which he communicated. As with most sources from decades ago, there are elements that are disconcerting if not offensive to modern readers. First among these is the use of masculine nouns and pronouns instead of inclusive language. Not changing that gendered language was a difficult decision, but ultimately, I agree with Luther Smith that Thurman's life and work bear witness to Thurman's belief in gender equality (e.g., his condemnation of the "man-dominated social order" and his support for the ERA in 1949)[11] and decided it was better not to alter Thurman's words.

Second, this book uses works that span decades. Although Thurman's thought was coherent and consistent over the course of his career, it also developed and changed. I tried to note aspects of this development, such as how, for example, Thurman's ideas about socialism, pacifism, and anti-imperialism were more radical in the 1930s during and after his trip to India but moderated some over the years.

THE PLAN OF THE BOOK

The thesis of this book is that Howard Thurman's interpretations of the Prodigal Son and Good Samaritan parables illustrate his understanding of how to (re)establish community with God (Prodigal Son) and therefore with other human beings (Good Samaritan). The book itself and the chapter study guides weave together major aspects of both my own and Thurman's interests that integrate responses to what these parables "mean," how they "work," and what they "want" from us in response: (1) in-depth exegesis of the parables themselves; (2) Thurman's insights into these parables and their implications; (3) the intersecting ways in which parables and visual art *work*, create a dialogue about their *meaning*, and encourage an *ethical response*; and (4) the ways in which parables and visual art can heighten spiritual consciousness and be used to create and deepen community.

Part 1 begins with chapter 1's examination of Thurman's life and career and an exploration of Thurman's classic book, *Jesus and the Disinherited*. Chapter 2 discusses Thurman's mysticism, its relationship with social change, and his practice of using the fine arts to raise one's spiritual consciousness, encourage a "sympathetic understanding" of other human beings, and deepen the sense of community.

Part 2 focuses on a painting by Rembrandt to illustrate the ways in which we should envision how parables "work" (chapter 3) and what parables "want" (chapter 4). Thurman correctly framed Jesus's message: Jesus spoke his parables in his own historical context as a poor, disinherited, oppressed, first-century Jew. He included trenchant critiques of the wealthy and powerful, and presented his answer to the disinherited and to the privileged: the Jewish love-ethic of loving God and one's neighbor—including the restoration of broken community—that are illustrated so forcefully by the parables of the Prodigal Son and the Good Samaritan.

In that light, part 3 and part 4 of this book have a twofold task. First, they attempt to understand better the parables of the Prodigal Son (part 3) and the Good Samaritan (part 4) in their first-century contexts. Second, using insights from Thurman, they make the two parables relevant for contemporary society without anachronizing or domesticating Jesus's message.

Part 3 argues that the Prodigal Son is a "parable about us" and includes Thurman's insights that one has to listen for the whisper of God and to recognize the sound of the genuine within us (chapter 5), with the conclusion that the prodigal's return and the differing receptions by his father and older brother illustrate that "there must be community" (chapter 6).

The demonstration of the father's love and compassion in the Prodigal Son parable is the pathway that leads to Thurman's interpretations of the Good Samaritan parable. Part 4 of the book (chapters 7, 8, and 9) thus interprets the parable of the Good Samaritan by arguing that the compassionate Samaritan can be seen as one of Thurman's "apostles of sensitiveness." In other words, the merciful Samaritan—just like the father in the Prodigal Son parable—models the compassion that Jesus shows for others, that Jesus proclaims God embodies, and that Jesus commands his followers to have for all human beings.

Part 5 (chapters 10 and 11) reaches some conclusions about Thurman's ideas about how human beings should strive to be transformed from being prodigals to becoming compassionate Samaritans. Just as the compassionate father in the Prodigal Son parable sets the standard for which human beings should strive, so does the compassionate Samaritan in the Good Samaritan parable. The responsibility for *restoring* community in response to their father, however, rests on the shoulders of both sons, just as responsibility for *extending* community, in response to the Samaritan, rests on the shoulders of the innkeeper. In this way, both parables place these responsibilities on the shoulders of all interpreters. Readers/hearers of these parables must decide how the sons and innkeeper should respond in ways that allow true community to emerge and expand—and readers/hearers should respond similarly in their own lives. The book concludes with thoughts about the way forward, including how "we all do better when we all do better" through compassion-in-action, justice, and extending community to all.

STUDY GUIDES FOR EACH CHAPTER

A teacher's guide that includes study guides for all eleven chapters of this book is found on the Paulist Press website: https://www.paulistpress.com/Pages/Center/quest-community-study-guides.aspx. The chapter study guides use visual art to, as Thurman envisioned, endeavor to increase understanding, raise spiritual consciousness, and deepen community. Each study guide contains (1) links to selected audios of Thurman's sermons and lectures relevant to the topic of the chapter; (2) reflections on or discussion questions about the visual art at the beginning of the chapter; (3) selected quotes from the chapter for reflection, interaction, and discussion; and (4) some additional information to aid teachers as they prepare for leading discussions about the chapter. The goal is that, by exploring and responding to what these parables want, we can continue the quest for common ground, for community, for, to paraphrase Thurman's words, "a friendly world of friendly human beings."

ACKNOWLEDGEMENTS

We are all of us indebted to a vast host by which we are surrounded.

Howard Thurman[1]

Researching and writing a book is in many respects a solitary project, but, as Thurman notes, all of us are indebted to a host of others, known and unknown. The following list of acknowledgements thus is a partial one, albeit hopefully representative of the vast host to whom I am indebted for this project.

Most of this book was written while on research leave from Oxford College of Emory University. I am grateful to Ken Anderson, then academic dean, for granting me a full-year sabbatical to work on this and other book projects. I had served as humanities division chair for four years and was scheduled for a sabbatical, but when the pandemic hit, I agreed to delay my sabbatical for two more years, so I much appreciated having a year that could be primarily dedicated to the writing of this book.

My position as Pierce Chair of Religion, one of the Distinguished Chairs of Emory University, provided the majority of funding for the research/writing travel for this book. I am also indebted to Tiffany Whitfield, administrative assistant for the Humanities Division and the Pierce Program in Religion, for expertly and graciously handling the financial records, the use of Pierce research funds, my travel, and many other details.

Research in the Howard Thurman & Sue Bailey Thurman Collections at Boston University's Howard Gotlieb Archival Research Center was supported by a University Research Committee Award from Emory University for my proposal, "Parables and Social Justice: Howard Thurman's Enduring Legacy." I am thankful for Jane Parr, archivist for acquisitions at Gotlieb, and the rest of the staff for their work in making those archival resources available to me during my visit to Boston in July 2022.

I was fortunate to spend August 2022 as a visiting professor and affiliate member in the School of Religious Studies, Faculty of Arts, at McGill University in Montreal, Quebec, Canada. I thank Sara Parks and Matthew Anderson for their many kindnesses and their assistance in making arrangements for our stay—including our wonderful apartment in Le Plateau-Mont-Royal—and Gerbern Oegema for sponsoring my visiting position at McGill. The time in Montreal was both restorative and productive, perhaps best illustrated by my many hikes up Mont Royal to sit in a chair outside Mont Royal Chalet to write about Howard Thurman's life (chapter 1), with the city of Montreal in front of me.

One of the most meaningful experiences for this project was a pilgrimage to Howard Thurman's boyhood home in Daytona Beach, Florida. Qasim Abdul-Tawwab, Howard Thurman Home site manager, hosted my tour, and Ms. Alberta Thomas, deaconess at Mt. Bethel Baptist Institutional Church and volunteer at the Howard Thurman Historic Home, arranged my visit to the church and a tour by its pastor, Eugene Hudson. The positive, mentoring aspects that Thurman mentions in his autobiography about his "church sponsors" and others in the church are clearly still evident today.

My sabbatical also provided opportunities that enhanced my understanding of liberation theology, Black theology, contextual theology, and other ways in which Thurman's legacy endures and progresses. For example, Pierce Chair in Religion research monies also funded a research/writing trip to Costa Rica, where the views of the Pacific Ocean from our roof patio as I wrote were just as inspirational as the views in Montreal. I am especially grateful to Elisabeth Cook, rector and professor of Hebrew Bible, at Universidad Bíblica Latinoamericana in San José, Costa Rica, both for hosting me at UBL and for our discussion of liberation theology in theory and practice in higher education.

Parts of chapters 3 and 4 of this book are significant revisions of what was published originally as "The Enthymematic Nature of Parables: A Dialogic Reading of the Parable of the Rich Fool (Luke 12:16–20)," *Review and Expositor* 109:2 (2012): 199–217.

Used with permission of *Review and Expositor* and SAGE Publications.

My initial explorations of the importance of the Prodigal Son and Good Samaritan parables in Howard Thurman's thought were published in two book chapters:

- "Sit and Listen; Go and Do: The Parables of the Good Samaritan and Prodigal Son in Howard Thurman's Life and Thought." Pages 434–51 in *Anatomies of the Gospels and Beyond the Gospels: Essays in Honor of R. Alan Culpepper*. E. J. Brill Biblical Interpretation Series 164. Edited by Elizabeth Struthers Malbon, Mikeal C. Parsons, and Paul N. Anderson. Leiden: E. J. Brill, 2018.
- "From Prodigals to Good Samaritans: One Path to Common Ground in Howard Thurman's Thought." Pages 50–65 in *The Unfinished Search for Common Ground: Reimagining Howard Thurman*. Edited by Walter Fluker. Maryknoll, NY: Orbis Books, 2023.

Most of the materials in those chapters used in this book are quotes from Thurman's sermons and other works, and I have footnoted any other references to those two chapters.

Thurman's observation, "We are all of us indebted to a vast host by which we are surrounded," reminds me of one of my favorite quotes from Mikhail Bakhtin, that the pursuit of "truth is not to be found inside the head of an individual person, it is born *between people* collectively searching for truth, in the process of their dialogic interaction."[2] Among the "vast host" with whom I have been in "dialogic interaction" include the multitude of scholars and students whose insights have informed my own and are reflected in this book's interpretations of the parables.

In particular, I am especially grateful to the three people who read the penultimate draft of this manuscript, Peter Eisenstadt, Nancy Gowler, and Luther Smith Jr., all of whom offered significant and helpful suggestions. All three have knowledge and experience in important aspects of this book, so their contributions made the book better, but, as always, any faults that remain are my own.

This book is the fourth that I have published with Paulist Press, the first two expertly and genially shepherded by †Lawrence Boadt, then president of the press. The professional and collegial atmosphere has continued under the leadership of Mark-David Janus, CSP, and I am especially grateful for all the others at Paulist Press who made this volume possible, including Paul McMahon, Donna M. Crilly, Mary Dern Walker, and Leah Arabia.

Among the vast host to whom this book is indebted are Howard Thurman and his family, including two of Thurman's grandchildren, Suzanne Mari Chiarenza and Anton H. Wong, who granted permission to publish sections of what I discovered in the archival materials at Pitts Theology Library, Howard Gotlieb Archival Research Center, the Thurman penguin painting in chapter 10, and other materials. My hope is that this book furthers the knowledge of and appreciation for Howard Thurman and his many contributions to the pursuit of truth. Thurman's work endures, and the dialogues with it move us forward.

The community to whom I am most indebted is my family whose love and support have been foundational: my parents, †Cedric and †Betty Gowler; my siblings, Rick, †Gary, and Nancy; and my wife Rita and our two sons, Camden and Jacob.

This volume I dedicate to the most important person in my life and my best friend. I dedicate this book about love, compassion, and community to Rita, because she epitomizes all three of those qualities that make each of us truly *human* in the best sense of the word.

Part I

Howard Thurman and the Religion of Jesus

1

"WITH THEIR BACKS AGAINST THE WALL"

Jesus of the People. © 1999 Janet McKenzie. www.janetmckenzie.com.
Rembrandt, *Head of Christ* (*Christuskopf*), 1645–1650, Berlin, Gemäldegalerie.

> I listened with wonderment, then anger, and finally mounting rage as Sam Cromarte preached my father into hell.
>
> Howard Thurman[1]

Seven-year-old Howard Thurman sat alongside his mother, Alice Ambrose Thurman, and grandmother, Nancy Ambrose, in the "mourners' bench," the front pew of Mount Bethel Baptist Institutional Church in Daytona, Florida, listening to Sam Cromarte preach the funeral sermon for Saul Solomon Thurman. As Thurman described it decades later,

> This was his chance to illustrate what would happen to "sinners" who died "out of Christ," as my father had done. And he did not waste it. Under my breath I kept whispering to Mamma, "He didn't know Papa, did he? Did he?"[2]

It was 1907, and Saul Thurman, who worked on a railroad crew laying track for the Florida East Coast Railroad, had come home sick with pneumonia. Thurman and his mother cared for him, as Saul Thurman, racked with fever, struggled to breathe. Thurman writes,

> He was the first person I had ever seen die. I was seven and my father was fifty-five. He had been sick only five days....Late in the afternoon of the fifth day, I stood with my mother beside his bed. At that moment his body was caught in a great spasm that lifted his large frame from the bed. We struggled to hold him down. Suddenly, it was all over. My father was dead.[3]

Thurman helped his mother and grandmother prepare the body for the funeral. He was then sent to ask their neighbors for the financial help the family needed to pay for the coffin, and their community, as always, supported them. The family faced other difficulties. As Thurman put it, although his mother was "a devout, dedicated praying Christian,"[4] Saul Thurman—a "good man"—was not a churchgoer; therefore, "in the eyes of the church he was a sinner." The pastor of the local Baptist church thus would not participate in the funeral. The family had to turn to a traveling evangelist in town, Sam Cromarte, to lead the funeral. Cromarte readily agreed, what Thurman initially thought was a "most gracious act" until in his sermon Cromarte used Saul Thurman as an object lesson to illustrate what happens to "unbelievers" and "sinners." Only during the long drive back from the cemetery was Thurman able to ask questions of his mother and grandmother:

> Why would Reverend Cromarte do this to Papa? Why would he say such things? Neither Mamma nor Grandma would answer my persistent query. Finally,

> almost to myself, I said, "One thing is sure. When I grow up and become a man, I will never have anything to do with the church."[5]

So begins the autobiography of Howard Washington Thurman, one of the foremost ministers, theologians, philosophers, and educators of the twentieth century. Despite this appalling early episode with organized Christianity, Thurman's brilliance, his many other gifts, and the supportive family and community in which he was raised led to what was to become a singular life and career, one in which what it meant to be a child of God and the quest for community would be paramount concerns.

FOOTPRINTS ON A PATH TO COMMUNITY: HOWARD THURMAN'S LIFE

Beginnings

Saul Thurman's death and funeral left deep scars in Thurman's psyche and alienated him from the church. Yet, by the time he reached his second year of high school, Thurman felt led to some sort of religious vocation. His decision to enter Christian ministry did produce a vague feeling that he was violating his father's memory, yet greater forces overcame this hesitancy. As Thurman's autobiography reveals, his decision to enter Christian ministry and the later successes in his life and career were in part possible because of the support he received from his family and his community, as well as the clear, insistent pull of the spirit of God within his own heart.[6]

Thurman's compassionate mother nurtured him with love and assured him, too, of God's love and protection. Thurman often mentions how when as a small child he was afraid after someone told him that Halley's Comet would fall from the sky, his mother comforted him, saying, "Nothing will happen to us, Howard. God will take care of us." This love, a sense of his worth as a child of God, and an understanding of the true teachings of Jesus were reinforced by his formidable grandmother, Nancy Ambrose, who was born (ca. 1844) into slavery in northern Florida. Thurman learned much about the religion of Jesus from her because she "had stood inside of Jesus and looked out on the world through his eyes."[7] In addition, his mother and grandmother taught him about a Christian experience—devotion to God and following Jesus—that was much broader than the teachings of their local church.[8]

The support of Thurman's family was strengthened and extended by members of the church and community in which he lived. Their lives were difficult, but the way of life in his neighborhood in good times and bad was: "We helped each other and we survived." Thurman later realized that despite his trauma at his father's funeral service, the watchful attention of his church sponsors served "to enhance my consciousness that whatever I did with my life *mattered*. They added to the security given to me by the quiet insistence of my mother and especially my grandmother that their children's lives were a precious gift."[9]

Family and community, then, were instrumental to Thurman's survival and flourishing, as were the distinctive spiritual experiences that he would later understand as (affirmation) mysticism, "a personal, private experience of Reality, of God" that includes a sense of community: "a unity not only with God but a unity with all of life, particularly with human life."[10] During his youth, for example, Thurman experienced a profound mystical spirituality through communion with nature, one that led him to sense the unity of all existence, and on which he later would build his sense of community. This sense of connection with nature included walks in quiet stillness along the Atlantic beach in which Thurman sensed that "all things, the sand, the sea, the stars, the night, and I were one lung through which all life breathed....I was a part of it and it was a part of me."[11]

These experiences, including the communion he felt with the live oak tree in his family's backyard,[12] drove Thurman to a more inclusive view of community, expanding beyond the confines of the traditional Christianity that "preached [his] father into hell."

Education

A brilliant student, Thurman graduated as valedictorian of his high school (1918), college (1923), and seminary (1926), even though he faced significant obstacles because of his race and economic status. For example, he was the first Black male child in Daytona to receive an eighth-grade certificate of graduation and, since there were only two public and six private high schools for Black people in the entire state of Florida, he had to attend high school at Florida Baptist Academy, about 110 miles away in Jacksonville.[13] He worked evenings to help pay for his room and board, worked eleven hours on Saturdays, and survived on eating just one meal a day.

Thurman received a scholarship to attend Morehouse College, a Black liberal arts college for men in Atlanta, Georgia. He enrolled in Morehouse in 1919 during what is called the "Red Summer" because of mostly white-on-Black violence in over three dozen U.S. cities. As Thurman noted of this time in Georgia, "Lynchings, burnings, unspeakable cruelties were the fundamentals of existence for black people. Our physical lives were of little value. Any encounter with a white person was inherently dangerous and frequently fatal."[14] The first twenty-three years of his life in Florida and Georgia left deep scars in Thurman's spirit, made him sensitive to the "churning abyss" between white and Black people, and impelled Thurman to devote his life "to the central concern that transcends the walls that divide" and his belief in the truth that all human life was one.[15]

Attending Morehouse significantly aided Thurman's personal and academic growth. In addition to studies, leadership positions, and extracurricular activities, Morehouse students were encouraged to strive toward excellence. His Morehouse teachers "placed over our heads a crown that for the rest of our lives we would be trying to grow tall enough to wear. This was a gift far greater than the imparting of information and facts."[16]

Thurman applied to Newton Theological Seminary in Newton, Massachusetts, but was denied because Black people were not admitted. He then applied to Rochester Theological Seminary (now Colgate Rochester Crozer Divinity School), which at that time accepted only one or two African American students a year. Thurman was accepted and for the first time lived in what he called "a totally white world."[17] Thurman felt himself a stranger, alienated from his surroundings in many ways.

Racism was usually less overt in New York than it was in Georgia or Florida, but Thurman became a focus of attention of the Ku Klux Klan in the area. Thurman was invited to speak in numerous local towns, and at one of those talks, racial resentment was so high that the threat of violence was clearly present as Thurman and the pastor who invited him walked a gauntlet of men lining the pathway to the church.[18]

Early Career

Thurman married Katie Kelley in 1926 and served as pastor at Mount Zion Baptist Church in Oberlin, Ohio. Because of Katie's diagnosis of tuberculosis, the Thurmans with their infant daughter Olive moved in 1928 to be near Katie's family in Georgia. Thurman returned to Atlanta to teach religion at Morehouse College and Spelman College. Katie died of tuberculosis in December 1930, and Thurman traveled in Europe that summer, mostly in solitude, to restore his spirit. He returned to the United States knowing "that I need never fear the darkness, nor delude myself that the contradictions in life are final. I was ready now for my journey."[19] That journey included a reintroduction to a friend, Sue Bailey, in the fall of 1931, and, on June 12, 1932, Thurman and Sue Bailey were married. That summer, the couple moved to Washington, DC, where Thurman began teaching at Howard University.

India, Gandhi, and a Transcendent Moment

From 1935 to 1936, Thurman was elected and served as chair of the "Negro Delegation" on a Pilgrimage of Friendship sponsored by the World Student Christian Movement. Thurman, Sue Bailey Thurman, and two other team members traveled to Ceylon (now Sri Lanka), Burma (now Myanmar), and India (including what is now Pakistan) on a nearly five-month-long preaching tour that included meeting with Mahatma Gandhi. They were the first African Americans to meet with Gandhi in India. During their three-hour meeting, Gandhi questioned them about the lives of African Americans in the United States in the contexts of slavery and continuing discrimination and then answered their questions about the difficulties Gandhi's movement faced in gaining independence from the British. Gandhi said that the masses of people, not just the leaders of the movement, needed to embrace *ahimsa*, the creative ethical ideal of nonviolence, but that many people were hindered by hunger, poverty, and "the loss of self-respect because of the presence of the conqueror in our midst." Then Gandhi explained that the main reason for this deficit in self-respect came from "the presence of untouchability in Hinduism," and he hoped that his efforts to build self-respect would help "to sustain a commitment to nonviolent direct action." Thurman writes that during the meeting Gandhi expressed his belief that "it could be through the Afro-American that the unadulterated message of nonviolence would be delivered to all men everywhere."[20]

Another transformative experience for Thurman during this trip was an early-morning hike up Tiger Hill to watch the sun rise over Kangchenjunga—a mountain in the eastern Himalayas. Thurman's description of his epiphany begins with an apt metaphor of the process of achieving clarity of vision:

> It was completely dark....At first there was just a faint finger of pink in the sky, then suddenly the whole landscape burst into one burnished gold radiance: everything was clear....The glorious sight lasted no more than a minute; the clouds came together again and closed the view.
>
> More than forty years have passed since that morning. It remains for me a transcendent moment of sheer glory and beatitude, when time, space, and circumstance evaporated and when my naked spirit looked into the depths of what is forbidden for anyone to see. I would never, never be the same again.[21]

Fellowship Church and Additional Recognition

In 1944, Thurman left his tenured position at Howard to serve as copastor of an interfaith and interracial church in San Francisco, California, the Church for the Fellowship of All Peoples. The name of the church denotes its mission of creating, in

Thurman's words, "a religious fellowship worthy of transcending racial, cultural, and social distinctions."[22]

In his pastoral role, Thurman was primarily concerned with the spiritual development of those who gathered for worship, which he believed should result in a deepening of community and in personal and social transformation. His sermons, for example, engaged with fundamental realities of human and religious experience and translated those realities into practical messages his congregation could apply. They also challenged his listeners to understand that community entails working for social justice.

Already a nationally and internationally recognized figure, Thurman's fame and influence continued to grow. In 1953, for example, *Life* magazine hailed Thurman as one of the twelve "Great Preachers" in the United States: "the country's most eminent preachers...shaping the spiritual life of America."[23]

Boston University and Retirement

Thurman devoted nine years to Fellowship Church and was certain that he would finish his career there. In 1953, however, the president of Boston University, Harold Case, persuaded Thurman to join the university as Professor of Spiritual Resources and Disciplines and dean of Marsh Chapel, becoming the first African American to be dean of a chapel at a predominantly white university. Case asked Thurman "to develop in the chapel at Boston University the kind of inclusive religious experience that you have developed at the Church for the Fellowship of All Peoples."[24]

In his later years at Boston University, Thurman transitioned to a position as minister-at-large, continued to speak and publish extensively, and travel, including trips to Africa and Israel. Thurman retired in 1965, and he and Sue Bailey Thurman returned to San Francisco, where Thurman directed the Howard Thurman Educational Trust until his death in 1981.

Although Thurman never considered himself a "movement man,"[25] he provided some of the key theological foundations of the civil rights movement. Thurman's influence, for example, is likely seen in Martin Luther King Jr.'s incorporation of Gandhi's nonviolent resistance with the religion of Jesus.[26] He also served as mentor to many key figures in the civil rights movement, directly and indirectly, helping to pave the spiritual path upon which King and others would tread. Thurman's classic book *Jesus and the Disinherited* served as a foundational text for many civil rights leaders and was a book that Martin Luther King Jr. often carried with him on his journeys.[27]

THURMAN, CHRISTIANITY, AND THE RELIGION OF JESUS

After Thurman's sojourn in India in 1935 to 1936, he described his ministry as "an exploration of the problems that arise in the experience of people who attempt to be Christian in a society that is essentially un-Christian."[28] This exploration would lead him to write his best-known book, *Jesus and the Disinherited*. In that book, Thurman observes that historical Christianity differs from the religion of Jesus in fundamental and troubling ways: Jesus primarily spoke to those oppressed by the powerful, and his prophetic message continues to be relevant to the oppressed in any age in ways not understood, acknowledged, or accepted by many who claim to follow him. Thurman's reflections on the African American experience in the United States, as well as on Jesus and the first-century Jewish experience, drove him to understand more clearly "what it really meant to be a Christian."[29]

In his autobiography, Thurman relates a story from his trip in Colombo, Sri Lanka, where a man asked how Thurman could represent Christianity to the people of Sri Lanka when his ancestors had been enslaved by Christians in North America and Black people continue to be "brutalized, lynched, burned, and denied most civil rights by Christians." The man considered Thurman to be "a traitor to all of the darker peoples of the earth." Thurman's reply is indicative of a position he continued to develop throughout his career:

> It is far from my purpose to symbolize anyone or anything. I think the religion of Jesus in its true genius offers me a promising way to work through the conflicts of a

> disordered world. I make a careful distinction between Christianity and the religion of Jesus. My judgment about slavery and racial prejudice relative to Christianity is far more devastating than yours could ever be.

The teachings of Jesus, Thurman argues, provide a creative solution to a disinherited minority struggling to survive, but Christianity became an imperial, world religion much different from the religion of Jesus, the Galilean teacher and prophet. As a result, the disinherited minority in the United States of which Thurman was a member should be dedicated to the teachings of Jesus, which are "on the side of freedom, liberty, and justice for all people."[30]

Thurman and the Religion of Jesus in Context

Life for African Americans in the United States—including his own experiences of discrimination and oppression—led Thurman to reflect deeply on how members of any despised and subjugated minority could not just survive but thrive: "Survival meant fashioning a creative response to one's environment, trying to shape it rather than merely being shaped by it."[31] The 1935 Good News for the Underprivileged lecture series, for example, begins with the key question, "What is the message, the good news, that Christianity has to give the poor, the disinherited, the dispossessed?"[32] Jesus was a Jew born in poverty, a "member of a minority race, underprivileged and to a degree disinherited," and unlike the more economically advantaged Paul, not a Roman citizen. Whereas Paul, who counseled obedience to governmental authorities and the reverent service of slaves to their masters, could appeal to Caesar when he was mistreated, Jesus could not. If a Roman soldier kicked Jesus into a Galilean ravine, he was merely a poor Jew in a ravine. In that context, Jesus offers to other poor disinherited Jews "*a technique of survival for a disinherited minority*." Jesus's message assures the disinherited that they are children of God and therefore they should believe in their inherent worth and that of all other human beings, who are also children of God.

Thurman's quest for the historical Jesus was a quest for the true religion of Jesus and its meaning for today, different from the Christianity that claimed but failed to follow Jesus. This Christianity of the privileged and powerful had little to offer the disinherited except empty words about being content in their status and focusing on their heavenly reward.[33] According to Thurman, Jesus is not to be worshipped as savior or as an object of devotion—Christians should worship *God*—but is instead an example to be emulated. For instance, Jesus supplies a model for activists willing to risk everything to pursue social justice and true community in the face of evil.[34]

JESUS AND THE DISINHERITED

"The significance of the religion of Jesus to people who stand with their backs against the wall has always seemed to me to be crucial."[35] These opening words of *Jesus and the Disinherited* state Thurman's major premise and address a serious gap in most New Testament scholarship—dominated by white males—by connecting the life and teachings of Jesus with all the disinherited who similarly stand with their backs against the wall, to provide them with "profound succor and strength." One reason for this gap in scholarship is that the religion of Jesus, "born of a people acquainted with persecution and suffering," had been transformed into a world religion of civilizations who maintained their position through a "ruthless use of power applied to weak and defenseless peoples"—the opposite of the religion of Jesus. Since most people consist of the poor, the disinherited, and the dispossessed, the question of what the religion of Jesus says to them is "perhaps the most important religious quest of modern life." The answer is found in the religion of Jesus illuminated by an understanding of his era and contexts: (1) Jesus of Nazareth was a *Jew* from Palestine, and the Christian church has tended to overlook Jesus's Jewishness; (2) Jesus was a *poor* Jew (e.g., in Luke 2:24, his parents gave the offering designated for the poor; cf. Lev 12:8); (3) Jesus was a member of an oppressed minority group who suffered under the rule of the Romans and rulers such as Herod the Great who exploited the people and extracted vast sums from them, pushing them further into a bare subsistence level. Jesus's message stemmed from the fact that he was a spiritual genius but also from the historical, economic, religious, and social contexts in which he lived.[36]

How can people survive in such a tenuous position? Jesus's teaching and ministry supply a response. He rejects both capitulation and armed resistance to the oppressor and offers another form of resistance that starts with the position that "the Kingdom of Heaven is in us."[37] Jesus incorporates the "profoundest ethical insight" of his Jewish faith, one also found in previous prophets in Israel, and proclaims the good news to the oppressed that fear, deception, and hatred—"the three hounds of hell that track the trail of the disinherited"—should no longer have dominion over them. Jesus, in other words, offers "a technique of survival for the oppressed."[38]

Jesus's social position was the same as the dispossessed and disinherited of every age, and Thurman points directly to the African American experience in the United States in his own era; African Americans were still not guaranteed their rights as citizens, lived under constant threats of violence, and had their backs continually against the wall. The answer, Jesus proclaims, is to reject fear, dishonesty, and hatred, and to act with love toward all, even your enemies, which demonstrates the humanity, power, and freedom of the disinherited.[39]

Thurman discusses three "hounds of hell" before devoting a chapter to the meaning and applicability of Jesus's Jewish love-ethic. "*Fear* is one of the persistent hounds of hell that dog the footsteps of the poor."[40] The fear of the economically and socially insecure arises out of helplessness from the one-sided violence they constantly face. This fear degrades their self-worth and dignity: it is devastating to know and to be constantly reminded that you do not count. The segregation and other effects of Jim Crow laws, enforced by violence or the threat of it, are but one modern example, and they are defended and maintained by those who call themselves Christians.

Fear can serve as a protection against violence—such as deciding that "flight" (or avoidance) is better than "fight" as a response—but Thurman argues that the religion of Jesus supplies another mode of response for the disinherited. For example, in his inaugural sermon in Nazareth (Luke 4:16–22), Jesus offers good news to the poor, deliverance to captives, and liberation for the oppressed. God knows you better than you know yourself, loves you, cares for you, and will supply you with what you need (e.g., Matt 10:28–31). This gives the disinherited a self-confidence in their worth, a new courage and power. Thurman notes that realization of one's self-worth as a child of God "is not enough, but without it, nothing else is of value. The first task is to become immunized against the most radical results of the *threat* of violence. When this is accomplished, relaxation can take the place of churning fear."

Realizing one's true self-worth answers a second basic question of the disinherited: "What am I?" The self-appraisal of one's infinite worth as a child of God leads to a more accurate appraisal of one's own "intrinsic powers, gifts, talents, and abilities" that is no longer affected by the lenses of the oppressors and allows one to transcend and remove the limitations placed upon them.[41]

The essence of the religion of Jesus is the realization "that God cares for me!" Although life is still hard—"as hard as crucible steel"—the child of God gains faith and awareness to "overcome fear and transform it into the power to strive, to achieve, and not to yield."[42]

Deception is perhaps the oldest technique used throughout the ages by the dispossessed to protect themselves from the powerful.[43] Thurman explores three basic options concerning deception:

1. The dispossessed are defeated before they start. In an unequal society, without real community, the disinherited's use of a facile insincerity with those wielding power over them is taken for granted. The powerful assume such insincerity—deception in fact can strengthen the discriminatory system—and the dispossessed use it to gain whatever meager political, economic, and social rights they can. Yet, Thurman argues, a lie "tends to destroy whatever sense of ethical values the individual possesses." People who live by lies tend to become lies and "the moral mercury of life is reduced to zero."[44]
2. The dispossessed may decide to deceive others only when their lives are in danger. Thurman finds this approach more challenging to critique, because people who live under constant threat "exert supreme

effort into just keeping alive." Yet deception cheapens life even within the marginalized group in interactions with one another.[45]

3. Thurman recommends a third option: complete and devastating sincerity, speaking simple, direct truth whatever the cost. Thurman, like Jesus and Gandhi, was aware of possible negative consequences but was optimistic about the overall result: "For the individual who accepts this, there may be quick and speedy judgment with attendant loss. But if the number increases and the movement spreads, the vindication of the truth would follow in the wake. There must always be the confidence that the effect of truthfulness can be realized in the mind of the oppressor as well as the oppressed."[46]

Thurman thus argues that the disinherited should always speak the truth. Thurman also argues that although sincerity itself is not a direct defense against the powerful, the presence of overwhelming sincerity among the disinherited leaves the oppressors no defense of their actions, and the relationship can be transformed from oppressor/oppressed into a relationship between human beings.

Hate is the final hound of hell.[47] Human beings can only empathize when they have sympathetic understanding—the ability to see themselves in another's place. The powerful, however, usually have an unsympathetic understanding that has limited knowledge of the other, and "contacts without fellowship" manifest themselves in actions of ill will that culminate in hatred of the disinherited by the "inherited."

This hatred, however, flows in both directions: the often-bottled bitterness of the disinherited leads to hatred of their oppressors, a hatred born out of a "systematic denial of the rights and privileges that are theirs, by virtue both of their being human and of their citizenship." Hate provides a rallying point, a source of energy, cunning, endurance, and a false sense of righteousness, an illusion that allows the disinherited to defend themselves as well as to justify operating in the lex talionis system without losing moral self-respect.[48]

Hate supplies the disinherited a basis for moral justification, inextricably involved in their complex techniques of survival against their oppressors. But Jesus, although he knew such hatred of the Romans could not be easily dislodged, still proclaimed, "Love your enemies and pray for those who persecute you" (Matt 5:43–48).

Thurman argues that the logic behind Jesus's love-ethic is that hatred

> destroys finally the core of the life of the hater. While it lasts, burning in white heat, its effect seems positive and dynamic. But at last it turns to ash, for it guarantees a final isolation from one's fellows. It blinds the individual to all values of worth, even as they apply to himself and his fellows. Hatred bears deadly and bitter fruit.

Hatred cannot be controlled once it is set in motion, and it spreads beyond just the oppressors who initially are its sole object.

Love is the foundation of the religion of Jesus, which centralizes the love-ethic in Jewish law: The love of God and the love of neighbor as oneself are the two greatest commandments. This love-ethic extends to all people by responding "directly to human need across the barriers of class, race, and condition." Jesus thus stood firmly within Judaism and envisioned himself a "creative vehicle" for its "authentic genius."

Thurman then argues that Jesus provides concrete examples of how to love different groups of enemies: (1) personal, (2) those who shame or humiliate you, and (3) oppressors. Loving the oppressor is extremely difficult, both in the wider social context and on a personal level, because such human-to-human contacts must transcend established roles and create a shared, common environment so all can participate as persons of equal status, worth, and value—"love is possible only between two freed spirits." This transformation—which for Thurman includes the overcoming of "white necessity" (sometimes called today "white privilege") and white supremacy—can only occur with a discipline, a method, a technique for working out a serious plan of implementation. Such efforts take the will to implement them, as well as painstaking discipline, and the process is more difficult for the disinherited because of the painful and often gratuitous injuries that come at the hands of their oppressors. Thurman believes, however, that the disinherited can forgive, since they have received the forgiveness of God, that no evil deed represents the full intention of the doer, and that "the evildoer does not go unpunished." For Thurman, the love of enemy assumes the underlying unity of life and that the contradictions of life—the evil that exists in the world—are not final.

CONCLUSION

More than seven decades after its publication, *Jesus and the Disinherited* remains a classic yet still underappreciated work with crucial insights. Although not a biblical scholar, Thurman was steeped in the biblical scholarship of his day, and advances in scholarship over the intervening decades both affirm and adjust Thurman's understanding of Jesus's first-century contexts. Moreover, Thurman's view of Judaism was both informed and enlightened: Christian scholars have tended to denigrate Judaism in their attempts to elevate Christianity. Thurman correctly repudiated that position and worked to portray Judaism accurately. Thurman also identified with the Jewish people and their sufferings—both in Jesus's day and his own—and recognized Jews and African Americans as similarly marginalized minority groups; the Jewish community had suffered segregation, violence, and persecution for centuries.[49]

Jesus and the Disinherited built a bridge from the first century to the twentieth—and now to the twenty-first—but the vast differences between those contexts still create a significant chasm. Jesus of Nazareth, for example, had no possibility of participating in the politics of his day and was speaking within Judaism and mostly to fellow disinherited Jews. Over the centuries, most interpreters have thought that his approach was too optimistic and unrealistic to be practical on a personal or, especially, societal level. Similar objections can be raised about Thurman's perspective, including the need for greater attention on justice and shifting more of the burden for societal change from the disinherited to the inherited. As Luther Smith notes, however, the latter criticism is misplaced. Thurman does not offer the inherited a loophole that lessens their burden or responsibility; instead, he offers a message of empowerment for the disinherited who are children of God whether or not their oppressors change their beliefs and behavior: "One does not have to wait for a confession or an apology or changes in behavior. Waiting for these outcomes keeps the initiative for healing with the enemy. An individual has the agency to be freed from bitterness and hatred by choosing to forgive—even if the process of forgiveness requires considerable effort and time."[50] Individuals have the responsibility and the means, Thurman said, to "trouble the waters," to provide a "shock to the system," to stimulate change.

Thurman makes clear that the demands of Jesus challenge us to change our perspective, orientation, and actions toward other human beings. Can we glean, as Thurman did, insights into how we can fruitfully implement Jesus's perspective?

2

THURMAN'S VISION OF ESTABLISHING COMMUNITY

Max Beckmann, German, 1884–1950; *Christ and the Sinner*, 1917; oil on canvas; 58 3/4 x 49 7/8 inches; Saint Louis Art Museum, Bequest of Curt Valentin 185:1955.

> There is no thing that does not have within it as part of its essence, the imprimatur of God, the Creator of all.... In all these things there is a secret door which leads to the central place, where the Creator of life and the God of the human heart are one and the same.
>
> Howard Thurman[1]

From his childhood, Thurman had been searching for common ground, for community. He elaborates on his belief in our mutual interdependence in his 1973 book *The Search for Common Ground*: "In human society, the experience of community, or realized potential, is rooted in life itself because the intuitive human urge for community reflects a characteristic of all life."[2]

THE UNITY OF LIFE AND COMMUNITY

Key to understanding Thurman's vision of community is his belief in the unity of all things. That belief, in part, is grounded in his communion with nature, such as his boyhood experiences walking along the shore of the Atlantic Ocean or sitting under the oak tree in his backyard. Another defining moment occurred in India during a private meeting with Dr. Kshitimohan Sen ("Singh" in Thurman's autobiography), a professor at the university in Shantiniketan in West Bengal, India. They spent the morning sparring verbally from their own religious perspectives, a Hindu and a Christian, and then realized what they were doing. So that afternoon, they started again in an effort to encounter each other as human beings, and Thurman observes,

> That afternoon I had the most primary, naked fusing of total religious experience with another human being of which I have ever been capable. It was if we had stepped out of social, political, cultural frames of reference, and allowed two human spirits to unite on a ground of reality that was unmarked by separateness and differences. This was a watershed experience in my life. We had become a part of each other even as we remained essentially individual. I was able to stand secure in my place and enter into his place without diminishing myself or threatening him.[3]

In essence, that type of community is one that Thurman would seek to create, foster, and maintain throughout his life, teaching, and ministry, a community that was not limited to or derivative from a particular religion. For Thurman, community is rooted in the order of the cosmos, not in a specific religious tradition, and the cosmos demands that relationships between human beings and between God and human beings "be one of harmony, integration, wholeness, all that we mean by love."[4]

Thurman claims that "the underlying unity of life seems to be established beyond doubt."[5] He points to the "basic structural patterns of nature," for example, to argue that all life has a fundamental unity. Community, above all, represented order, a living, natural, and divine ordering.[6] The concern for wholeness thus is an essential intent of life.

Community is characterized by people recognizing their self-worth and acting on their purpose for life. As Luther Smith notes, for Thurman, "Community is salvation; it is life at its highest level," and it is "God's signature on everything in creation."[7] This sense of Oneness—the underlying unity of reality—is what God desires for all of creation. Human beings should live their lives in accord with such unity, and this unity—true community—is the end purpose of life. Reconciliation, then, is virtually synonymous to love in Thurman's estimation, with the definition of love being "the intelligent, kindly but stern expression of kinship of one individual for another, having as its purpose the maintenance and furtherance of life at its highest level."[8] Love both works to complete the fragmented, unfulfilled individual and reconciles and connects human beings: if "community is to be established, love must be the prevailing ethos of all relationships."[9]

MYSTICISM AND SOCIAL CHANGE

> Thurman's concentration on the plight of the oppressed and disinherited, his concern for a social order governed by the love-ethic, and his vision of the inclusive community...[do] not condone the present political and social realities, but [they feel as] a religious imperative to transform these realities.
>
> Luther Smith[10]

Thurman believed that true community could be created in two steps. First, the individual experiences a kinship with God—

becoming aware of the unity of all life—and experiences community personally. Second, community is experienced through establishing relationships encouraged and sustained by love: "Love transforms isolated and apathetic lives into related and caring ones."[11] If you love God with all your heart, mind, and strength, it necessarily follows that you love your neighbor as yourself. Love sustains all things and builds true community. Therefore, "if we accept the basic proposition that all life is one, arising out of a common center—God, all expressions of love are acts of God."[12]

In "Mysticism and the Experience of Love," Thurman's working definition of *mysticism* is "the response of the individual to a personal encounter with God within his own spirit."[13] In Thurman's view, the experience of God is fundamental, grounded in a transcendent unity. That unity can be experienced mystically, leading inevitably to positive social engagement. Truth must be experienced, but what is grasped through spiritual insight could be made secure with logic and rational thought, with mystical experiences being continually questioned and tested.[14] As the title of Thurman's autobiography illustrates—*With Head and Heart*—religious experience (the heart) thus affirms knowing the world, and rational thought (the head) examines and weighs that mystical experience. Thurman's affirmation mysticism thus envisions an expanding process of interactions that result in transformations of the social order (see chapter 9).

The initial step is a mystical experience in which the individual encounters the divine in a personal way, one that affirms the person's ultimate worth as a child of God, provides glimpses into the levels of reality, and results in a commitment. God is the Absolute to which one's life is fully surrendered and devoted. This experience and commitment transform the character and habits of the individual, provide that individual with new emotional, spiritual, and physical power to respond to the vicissitudes of life, and generate a desire to be Godlike and to express fuller meanings of love. The latter necessarily involves seeking to change the social order, because in their efforts to achieve what is good, individuals discover that they "must be responsive to human need by which [they are] surrounded, particularly the kind of human need in which the sufferers are victims of circumstances over which, as individuals, they have no control."[15]

This transformation of self and society creates community, as individuals respond to the vision of God and establish the interpersonal and societal environments in which the love-ethic is foundational and normal.[16] The child of God realizes others as children of God and seeks to cultivate relatedness with others; out of that sense of relatedness emerges community.[17]

MYSTICISM AND CIVIL RIGHTS

Civil rights is one of the many social implications of Thurman's affirmation mysticism, as found in Thurman's 1966 essay, "Desegregation, Integration, and the Beloved Community."[18] Thurman notes that only a revolution would break up the foundation of a society in which segregation was so entrenched and racial inequality so vigorously defended by the powerful. Desegregation, Thurman argues—the mere absence of segregation—is superficial change, whereas true integration, as opposed to *token* integration (e.g., the presence of a small number of members of an underrepresented group in an otherwise unchanged institution), means "to unify, to combine, to become whole, to become one."[19] Such unity may be encouraged by changes in policies and regulations, but unity has to "emerge as an experience after the fact of coming together." In other words, as Thurman discovered in his experiences with Fellowship Church, the mere presence of people of different ethnic or cultural backgrounds did not mean the church was integrated. True integration developed from unifying experiences that were multiplied over extended periods of time. Integration could begin to create a beloved community, defined by "the quality of the human relations experienced by the people who live within it....It cannot be brought into being by fiat or by order; it is an achievement of the human spirit as men seek to fulfill their high destiny as children of God."[20]

In the face of such powerful adversaries, many people were pessimistic that a beloved community could be achieved because of the "vast decay of our diseased, prejudiced-ridden society." Thurman declares, however,

> I disagree with this position utterly. The presence of the beloved community is always manifesting itself in

> the lives of people in the very midst of the social decay by which they are surrounded....
>
> At long last, what is being sought is a way of life that is worth living and a faith in one's self, in others, and in the society that can be honestly and intelligently sustained.[21]

Thurman's affirmation mysticism thus is fundamentally optimistic; it was a "deep optimism arising out of the pessimism of life."[22] Similar to his discussion of hate in *Jesus and the Disinherited*, Thurman was convinced that cynicism, alienation, and isolation were self-defeating and self-negating luxuries that those with their backs against the wall could not afford. Thurman's optimism did not deny life's many difficulties, especially for the disinherited, but he saw religion—exemplified by the religion of Jesus—as the path for seeking the truth of God in a world full of pain.[23]

In contrast, Thurman argues, people who believe that such contradictions are final or ultimate end up despairing, and in effect evading or denying their responsibilities for moral actions.[24] Thurman realizes—in part because of the racial oppression he endured—the difficulties involved in building a beloved community, and he also cautions about the "soft and sentimental ring" the term conjures. A beloved community still has disagreements, disputes, and conflicts, but it works diligently toward equality:

> It is a society where no artificial barriers separating man from man or groups from one another—where the precious ingredient in each personality, unique unto itself, may be so honored by his fellows that it will enrich the common life even as it creates its own light in which to stand....There [will] be new forms and patterns emerging, the blending of which will give to the society as a whole a richness and stimulation that will make for the general health and well-being. Disagreements and conflicts will be real and germane to the vast undertaking of man's becoming at home in his world and under the eaves of his brother's house.[25]

Thurman, even in times of despair, did not give up hope, because "of the awareness of the potential in me, in other people, in life itself" and the possibility of the mutual sharing of worth with other human beings.[26] To succeed, however, the dominant characteristic in human relationships should be *love*, not a sentiment or emotion but "the truest and most dependable tie that binds me to my fellows and them to me."[27]

THE ROLE OF THE FINE ARTS IN BUILDING COMMUNITY

> [William Blake] was always trying to see something and get at something and express something that other people didn't quite see and express, and he was forthright and direct and honest so one need not be surprised that his life was involved in a series of explosions of one kind or another.
>
> Howard Thurman[28]

The importance Thurman gives to the role of fine arts in building community can be illustrated by who he featured in his two-lecture series—the first series in 1950 and the second series in 1953—titled, "Men Who Have Walked with God." Those sermons focused on some of his favorite mystics, including Saint Francis, the Buddha, Lao-Tse, Mahatma Gandhi, Jane Steger, and Meister Eckhart. Tellingly, Thurman includes artists among these mystics, such as William Blake and Fra Angelico. The sermon on Blake is just one example of Thurman's recognition that artistic expression—visual art, music, dance, theater, film—can stimulate heightened spiritual consciousness and bring diverse people together on common ground.

Blake was an English poet, printmaker, painter, and radical Christian mystic whose work is original, independent, and prophetic.[29] Blake's poetry and images stem from his visionary, supernatural impulse (e.g., his "Genius" or "angel"), and he speaks of the "doors of perception" in his book *The Marriage of Heaven and Hell*, the dialogic nature of art that engages its viewers/readers/hearers in perceiving infinite reality. Thurman admired Blake, viewing him as a fellow traveler who, similar to Thurman, "saw the unity of all living things as representing a lost original unity."[30]

Thurman recognizes that Blake had a vision of the "inner" and the "outer" that allowed Blake to see the underlying unity of all living things: "The outer was merely that through which he looked at the inner." Thurman states,

> When I look at you I do not see you. Your name is an externality, your features are external, even your little world of thinking is external. When I see you, when I look through the visible to the invisible, I come upon what? I come upon the same essence that is I. When in my behavior I deal with you on that theory then the brotherhood becomes but the human expression of the basic underlying external unity that connects all creation.[31]

Thurman elaborates on how this kinship can be achieved or, as he calls it, the "working out of redemption." One key aspect that Blake illustrates is the necessity of sacrificing one's ego:

> So when I love you, and because of my love for you, I must relax some crucial and important aspect of my self-regarding impulses....All of life becomes a process by which I overcome all the barriers that separate me from you.[32]

Luther Smith observes that the aims of Thurman's innovations involving art and meditation were twofold. They were designed (a) to help evoke religious experiences that "magnified the essence of religion" as opposed to dogma and (b) to affirm and facilitate unity within a religiously, socially, and philosophically diverse congregation.[33] In other words religious experience—the "conscious and direct exposure of the individual to God"—could be activated by one's inner awareness or by the contemplation of nature, worship, ideas, or art, including recurring experiences and relationships with other human beings that are characterized by love.[34]

The ways in which Thurman believed that fine arts could help raise such spiritual consciousness and assist in building community are first seen in his explorations of African American spirituals.

THE SPIRITUALS: A DEEP RIVER AND A GROUND FOR HOPE

To stay in the field
To stay in the field
Until the war is ended.

Black spiritual "Stay in the Field"[35]

In Black spirituals, Thurman saw a "ground of hope and self-respect." Thurman spoke about the spirituals—a touchstone of his own faith—as early as 1925, but his first "formal statement" about the spirituals came in a series of five addresses in the Spelman College chapel in the fall of 1938.[36] As he notes in the introduction to a 1975 reprinting of the combined edition of his two books on the spirituals, *Deep River and The Negro Spiritual Speaks of Life and Death*, "These essays are intimate and personal. They lay bare in my hand the gift which these songs, centuries old, are to my own spirit. For me, they are watering places for my own spirit and have enabled me to affirm life when its denial would be more ego satisfying, to honor my own heritage and rejoice in it." Thurman then closes with the quote from above, indicating that he was able "to stay in the field."[37]

From where did people creating and singing the spirituals gain the strength to endure their enslavement with all its terrors and suffering? Thurman states, "The awareness of the presence of a God who was personal, intimate and active was the central fact of life and around it all the details of life and destiny were integrated."[38] The focus on heaven in these spirituals was not "purely a mechanism for escape." Although it served to raise the capacity for endurance of enslaved people through their suffering, "this total experience enabled them to reject annihilation and affirm a terrible right to live. Their *center of focus* was beyond themselves in a God who was a companion to them in their miseries even as He enabled them to transcend their miseries."[39]

This relationship with God made what others considered a worthless life, life as chattel property, "*worth living*"; they were children of God, known by name by the creator of the universe.[40] Thurman thus argues that it was out of this sense, this *certainty*, of being a child of God "that the genius of the religious folk songs is born."[41] As Thurman writes, "this is the God in man," and it gave the people strength to persevere, a complete refusal to be stopped, and a resourcefulness enabling them to transform "the spear of frustration into a shaft of light."[42] As a spiritual puts it,

> I got wings,
> You got wings,
> All God's children got wings.[43]

This understanding, sung in the spiritual "Heaven, Heaven!" ("Heab'n, Heab'n!"), went beyond just a protest against the injustice of slavery to criticize hypocrisy and deception and to envision a time when true freedom and equality would come. This vision, Thurman argues, was based on the confidence that all human beings were equally children of God who could be in relationship with the creator of the universe. This confidence was a constant source of comfort and strength—and the first step toward true community.

THE FINE ARTS, HEIGHTENED CONSCIOUSNESS, AND COMMUNITY

The first aspect of the fine arts that led Thurman to incorporate them innovatively into worship services is how they help raise spiritual consciousness and receptiveness. In Thurman's view, for example, music played an integral role in liturgy, as did all fine arts, because this outward observance was a "ceremonial call to inwardness."[44] As Thurman noted, "Modern man, too often beset by sins and anxiety, desperately needs experiences that make for wholeness, for synthesis, for validation," what Thurman called the integrating moment.[45]

Thurman's book *Disciplines of the Spirit* provides examples of how fine arts can facilitate raising spiritual consciousness. He argues that "the true purpose of all spiritual disciplines is to clear away whatever may block our awareness of that which is God in us." Among the ways to achieve this end is the practice of silence, which takes many forms as, for example, Society of Friends' meetings illustrate (e.g., a prelude to prayer). After the calming of the mind has been achieved, the "real work" begins, and it can be accomplished by such practices as reading or recalling a passage, such as a psalm, a poem, or a picture that "speaks peace to the spirit at a time of great upheaval."[46] Thurman also utilized music selections that in his view assisted people to encounter and engage more deeply with the meanings of the passages they read.[47]

As Amanda Brown illustrates, Thurman creatively used the fine arts as a "readying method" in worship services at Fellowship Church as an avenue to heightened consciousness. Artistic expression is one way to prepare the mind for spiritual insight, and it was through this heightened spiritual consciousness that people—no matter their diverse backgrounds and experiences—could be brought together over common ground. Thurman understood that a key result of such heightened spiritual consciousness in worship could be a heightened sense of community. Thurman was convinced that repeated, significant experiences would overcome "preexisting ideas about human division and separateness."[48]

The fine arts are embodied; they involve aesthetic dimensions of the body through the senses—such as seeing, hearing, touching—and include emotions and cognition, feeling and knowing.[49] Thurman's worship experiences thus created liminal spaces in which community could be created again and again, a repetition that provided the embodied space where community could be sustained.

THE FINE ARTS AND CREATING A UNITY OF FELLOWSHIP

A key development in Thurman's vision of community is his experience near the end of his journey in India where he spent a day in Khyber Pass (now on the Pakistan/Afghanistan border). For Thurman, this experience confirmed the possibility of true human community:

> All that we had seen and felt in India seemed to be brought miraculously into focus. We saw clearly what

we must do somehow when we returned to America. We knew that we must test whether a religious fellowship could be developed in America that was capable of cutting across all racial barriers, with a carry-over into the common life, a fellowship that would alter the behavior patterns of those involved. It became imperative now to find out if experiences of spiritual unity among people could be more compelling than the experiences which divide them.[50]

This vision at Khyber Pass deepened Thurman's vision of true community that he would strive to achieve for the rest of his life and ministry. After his return from India, Thurman in his role as dean of Rankin Chapel at Howard University began to experiment with innovations to worship services that "would permit greater freedom for the play of creative imagination," such as extended times of meditation and vesper services that included dance. As Thurman notes in his autobiography, introducing dance as an act of worship in the 1930s was a daring if not hazardous experiment, but it resulted in a breakthrough of true community:

> Suddenly it was as if the walls separating each of us from the other were removed, and we became a worshipful people united by a single rhythmic beat. It was magnificent. Here was a young Caucasian woman, Roman Catholic by religious faith, sharing an experience of profoundest spiritual significance with a group made up of predominantly black Protestant worshippers in a university religious service. What happened was its own authenticity.[51]

Thurman writes similarly about the spiritual significance of another innovation at his Twilight Hours vesper services: a staged presentation of "Living Madonnas," where participants replicated six European masterpieces of visual art on stage while Ave Marias by various composers were played or sung. Thurman states that "the effect was electrifying" and notes how the congregation's heightened spiritual consciousness led to greater community among them:

> In the interval between each reproduction, there was utter silence; it was what [Rudolf] Otto calls "the numinous silence of waiting." The congregation and the participants were fused in a single moment of spiritual transcendence. I discovered again through worship, that an experience of unity among peoples can be more compelling than all that separates and divides.[52]

As Thurman explains in *Footprints of a Dream*, these innovations using the fine arts expanded during his time at Fellowship Church, where, for example, efforts to create a unity of fellowship through the fine arts included children's programs. Children were introduced to the "art, music, and artifacts" of other cultures such as songs, stories, handicrafts, worship materials, and games. In this way, children experienced all other peoples as real persons like themselves. Through such programs, Thurman attempted to promote spiritual experiences of unity and "to find a way to provide, to create, a religious commitment revealing the profound desire for community which would at the same time give room enough for honoring particular religious backgrounds in the lives of the people entering into the fellowship."[53]

Similar programs incorporating the fine arts also focused on the entire church "to expose the church members and their friends to the life, the culture, the hopes of people who have come from everywhere to form the corporate strength of American society." The fine arts were thus integral parts of religious experience and social fellowship of church members, and Thurman notes that a climate slowly emerged in the church "in which the fruits of culture could be appreciated, assimilated, and shared without patronage or condescension."[54]

In his autobiography, Thurman elaborates on the reasons why the fine arts were so critical for community at Fellowship Church. He writes that he believed that any goodwill people had for each other that "did not have as its center a hard core of fact and understanding was futile and mere sentimentality." Even with an ethnically and culturally diverse congregation, Thurman knew it was necessary to "thicken" their relationships and sought to deepen their intercultural fellowship and interactions in various ways. The fundamental question was whether these experiences could be programmed. Although Thurman didn't know the answer, he tested that idea at Fellowship Church, because he and Sue Bailey Thurman had

> a profound conviction that meaningful and creative experiences between peoples can be more compelling than all the ideas, concepts, faiths, fears, ideologies, and prejudices that divide them; and absolute faith that if such experiences can be multiplied and sustained over a time interval of sufficient duration *any* barrier that separates one person from another can be undermined and eliminated.[55]

At Howard University, Fellowship Church, Boston University, and elsewhere, Thurman discovered that through this approach to worship, "an experience of unity among peoples can be more compelling than all that separates and divides" and that such fellowship could lead to a "sympathetic understanding [that] often leads to the exercise of goodwill."[56] Again, in Thurman's view, heightened spiritual consciousness—exemplified in the Prodigal Son parable—can lead to the compassion-in-action illustrated in the Good Samaritan parable.

CONCLUSION: VISUAL ART AND THE PARABLES

As noted in Thurman's sermon on William Blake, he observes that Blake often had tempestuous relationships because "he was forthright and direct and honest."[57] Writing to a patron who had rejected one of his paintings,[58] Blake said,

> What is Grand is necessarily obscure to Weak men. That which can be made Explicit to the Idiot is not worth my care. The wisest of the Ancients considered what is not too Explicit as the fittest for Instruction because it rouzes the faculties to act.[59]

Blake's argument that what is not too explicit "rouzes the faculties to act" is a key component of this book's arguments: parables as works of art function in the same way that Blake envisioned visual works of art should "work": they "rouze the faculties to act."

Part II

How Do Parables Work? What Do Parables Want?

3

HOW DO PARABLES WORK?

Rembrandt, *The Money Changer* (*Der Geldwechsler*) or *The Rich Fool*, 1627, Berlin, Gemäldegalerie.

What then are the parables...? They are the natural expression of the mind that sees truth in concrete pictures rather than conceives it in abstractions.

C. H. Dodd[1]

My father loved parables—stories that taught, stories that presented ideas and morals in ways that made pictures in people's minds....Because he believed stories were so important as teaching tools.

Octavia Butler[2]

The room is dark, illuminated by a single candle. An elderly man sits at a desk overloaded with books and papers, some written in what appears to be Hebrew script. The man, a pince-nez perched on his nose, thoughtfully examines a coin. The hand holding the coin blocks the viewer from seeing the candle directly, but its glowing light illuminates the man, a small area of the desk, and other elements in the darkened room.

All inessential elements are cloaked in shadows. The man's face is brilliantly lit, and we see virtually every detail of his aged, wrinkled face as he gazes at the coin in his hand.[3] Other coins on the desk glimmer in the reflected glow of the candle's light.

Who is this man, and what does this painting say to its viewers? The image resists characterization, and it leaves many questions unanswered—even the subject of the work is disputed. Some scholars argue that it is a depiction of the Rich Fool parable in Luke 12:16–20, but the Gemäldegalerie in Berlin (correctly) titles it *The Money Changer* (*Der Geldwechsler*). Rembrandt clearly wants us to focus on the elderly man. He illuminates the man's face and mutes elements in the background. Rembrandt's manipulation of light and shadow, along with the man's seemingly introspective detachment, create a sense of mystery.

The painting is entrancingly engaging and enigmatic, just like Jesus's works of art, the parables. The rays of light in Rembrandt's work are reflected in various ways and sundry places, just as parables are reflected in different ways in different contexts and are heard in many ways by various hearers. Rembrandt illuminates some objects clearly, while other aspects remain murky or obscure, placed deliberately in the shadows, creating uncertainties and provoking debates. In a similar way, the parables of Jesus illuminate some things clearly; other aspects become clearer as we learn more about the first-century contexts in which Jesus created and his followers preserved, transmitted, and transformed his words. Other aspects, however, remain tantalizingly ambiguous. How can we explain the ways in which these enigmatic visual and literary works of art function?

JESUS'S PARABLES IN CONTEXT

Jesus was a pious first-century Jew who led a renewal movement within Judaism and debated with other first-century Jews how best to follow God, determine God's will, and observe God's law. Jesus's parables, as we find them in the Gospels, are distinctive but not unique. Since Jesus was a Jewish teacher and wonderworker, interpretations of his parables should incorporate as much as possible the contexts in which he created his parables and in which they were later preserved and developed. Parables were part of his teaching repertoire, and to understand better their use and function as well as the creative understanding involved in their construction, we must look at first-century cultural contexts in which these parables were spoken and heard. A fundamental aspect of parable interpretation involves the dialogues between what could be called the Jewish context and the larger Greco-Roman context. Although Jesus's Jewish heritage is essential—and dangerous anti-Jewish misinterpretations often result from ignoring or misrepresenting it—the larger Greco-Roman culture in which the Jewish people were embedded influenced first-century Judaism. In addition, although Jesus most likely taught primarily in Aramaic, the Gospels were written in Greek, and the Jesus of the Gospels speaks and acts in ways that combine Jewish and Greco-Roman modes of words and deeds.[4]

Jewish Contexts

The Greek word for parable (*parabolē*) is typically used to translate the more general Hebrew term *mashal* (plural: *meshalim*). By its very nature, *mashal* is difficult to describe and almost impossible to define, but its root meaning can be seen as "to represent" or "to be like."[5] In the Hebrew Bible, *mashal* usually includes a wider range of usage than does *parable* in the Gospels, although there are exceptions. Luke 4:23, for example, uses *parabolē* for the proverb, "Physician, heal thyself." None of the *meshalim* of the Hebrew Bible, though, are exact parallels to the New Testament's use of parable as a short narrative. Isaiah's *mashal* of the vineyard (Isa 5:1–6) might qualify as an allegorizing parable, but Nathan's story of the rich man slaughtering the lamb of a poor man that he tells David in 2 Samuel 12:1–6 is the closest to the narrative parable form that we find in the teachings of Jesus.

One meaning of *mashal* can be "riddle"—which means that the response of the hearer/reader is essential to the process of creating understanding about the possibly inferred meanings and implications of the *mashal*. Interpreters may or may not be able to understand the analogy or allusion being made; note how David misunderstood Nathan's *mashal* in 2 Samuel 12:1–6 and how Nathan had to interpret the *mashal* for David ("You are the man!" of 2 Sam 12:7–14).

Parables play a prominent role in later Jewish literature. Rabbis, for example, used them in a variety of contexts, such as preaching, interpreting Scripture, and providing guidance for daily living. *Meshalim* draw a series of parallels between the story recounted in the narrative and the "actual situation" to which the parable is directed. These parallels, however, are not drawn explicitly; the audience is left to derive them for themselves, which, like Nathan's *mashal*, can be confusing if the analogy or parallel is not clear enough. So, the parable is neither a simple tale with a transparent lesson nor an opaque story with a secret message; it is a narrative that actively elicits from its audience the interpretation and application of its message. The social context, then, can help to clarify the parable by giving the audience information they need to understand it, and, if the readers do not understand the social context, the parable can be even more difficult to understand. Jesus's parables, albeit earlier and in some ways distinctive (e.g., they tend to focus on rural culture and people), share a common background, composition, and form with rabbinic parables.[6]

Greco-Roman Contexts

Rhetoric was pervasive throughout Greco-Roman society by the first century CE, and rhetorical modes of argumentation saturated everyday discourse in almost every form of oral and written communication.[7] The most important rhetorical influences to the formation (and interpretation) of the Gospels are the *progymnasmata* (or "preliminary exercises"), compositional textbooks used in secondary education that represent widespread educational practice for those who read, spoke, and wrote Greek.[8] These rhetorical handbooks, such as the one by Aelius Theon of Alexandria (middle-to-late first century CE), instilled fundamental rhetorical skills to prepare students for more complex forms of oral and written composition, such as longer speeches and narratives.[9] The parables, as well as other elements of composition in the Gospels, reflect this rhetorical training.

In his influential 1886 book *Die Gleichnisreden Jesu*, Adolf Jülicher contended that "the majority of the *parabolai* of Jesus, the ones bearing a narrative form, are fables, such as the ones of Stesichoros and of Aesop."[10] Scholars such as T. W. Manson rejected this categorization by arguing that parables tend to depict human relations whereas fables are "pure fiction" that often invest animals, birds, and plants with human attributes.[11] In antiquity, however, the term *fable* denotes several kinds of brief narratives, including those stemming directly from human experience. Aelius Theon, for instance, defined *fable* more generally as "a fictitious story picturing a truth."[12]

Recent scholars have confirmed the connections between *fable* and *parable*. Mary Ann Beavis, for example, notes that students throughout the Roman Empire learned composition in the *progymnasmata* by hearing, reciting, and rewriting fables in their own words.[13] The authors of the Synoptic Gospels had at least a Greek elementary education, and they similarly shaped Jesus's parables as fables. Joshua Stigall built on Beavis's insights by examining the parable of the Rich Fool and concluding that Luke's construction of the parable is remarkably similar to Theon's teaching about fables, such as the way the parable is woven into a larger narrative, a moral is explicitly included (Luke 12:15, 21), and, in relation to the parable as it is found in the Gospel of Thomas, was expanded rhetorically.[14]

Mikeal Parsons and Michael Martin also provide confirmation that Jesus's parables exhibit the same literary features and practices as ancient fables.[15] Exercises on fable in the *progymnasmata* not only taught foundational literary skills through such practices as paraphrase, expansion and compression, and refutation and confirmation, all of which led to compositional mastery of the fable, but also sought to form character, inculcating cultural values, ethics, and morality in students.

A detailed examination of the fable tradition in particular and the Greco-Roman rhetorical tradition in general thus reveals that parables are indeed fables.[16] An Aesopic fable is even attributed to Jesus in the Gospel of Thomas 102: "Woe to the Pharisees, for they are like a dog sleeping in the manger of oxen; neither does he eat nor allow the oxen to eat."[17]

INTERPRETING PARABLES, FABLES, AND *MESHALIM*

For many interpreters, whether of fables, rabbinic parables, or the parables of Jesus, arriving at the meaning of the story is a primary goal. Like Rembrandt's *The Money Changer*, however, parables can be enigmatic and sometimes puzzling. A *mashal*, for example, can simplify a difficult or complex concept, but it also can be more esoteric. In other words, the parallels between the *mashal* and the "actual situation" to which it is directed can vary substantially in their explicitness, and the amount of transparency also can vary significantly.

Aesop's fables include an explicit moral at the end. The moral of the hare and the tortoise fable, for example, where the tortoise wins the race through a slow, steady pace because the overconfident speedy hare takes a nap, is often stated as "slow and steady wins the race." Rabbinic parables include an application just after the story. Fables illustrate for their hearers the way things are in life—and perhaps how things should be—with characters that exemplify, in either realistic or exaggerated forms, virtue and vice, right and wrong, and behaviors, actions, and attitudes that are therefore to be emulated or avoided. Similar morals or interpretations are included after (or before) parables in the Gospels, sometimes placed on the lips of Jesus; sometimes noted by the narrator. See, for example, Mark's version of the parable of the Sower (Mark 4:1–8) that includes Jesus's rather lengthy explanation of the parable to the twelve (4:10–20).

In fable collections, morals could be included before the fable, which serves as a way to "index" the fable by providing the subject matter or topic, or in the narrative after the fable, which applies the story to the situation in the overarching narrative. Prior to the parable of the Rich Fool in Luke 12:15, we read, "Take care! Be on your guard against all kinds of greed; for one's life does not consist in the abundance of possessions." The moral is found in Luke 12:21: "So it is with those who store up treasures for themselves but are not rich toward God." The first focuses on greed; the second is about having correct priorities.

The Midrash Song of Songs Rabbah (1.1, 8) recommends that interpreters not underestimate the *mashal*, since these apparently simple stories can be the gateway to understanding the law of God: "So the parable should not be lightly esteemed in your eyes, since by means of the parable a [person] arrives at the true meaning of the Torah." Similarly, Apollonius of Tyana praised fables by saying, "I find them more conducive to wisdom than the others." In his view, Aesop's fables use humble fictive incidents "to teach great truths" (*Life of Apollonius* 5.14). Greek fables were also valuable tools for instruction and persuasion. Fables/parables were commonly used in public speaking in the ancient world, a staple in formal and informal education, and, perhaps most importantly, often used to promote a particular ethical perspective.[18] Fables/parables require active engagement from their hearers or readers; they must decide, for example, which if any of the characters they should emulate to reach a similar outcome or to avoid it.

Multiple Morals, Meanings, and Applications

Even though an apparently universal moral could be appended to a fable—just as an apparently universal moral could be appended to rabbinic parables—the "originally lively fable" was not created "to convey a universal truth of general application." Instead, the fable is "the diplomatic intermediary of a wholly specific, acute truth that should directly encounter *a particular hearer* at *a particular point in time*, that should be effective immediately on *a particular concrete occasion*."[19]

This aspect of parables/fables means that on one hand, the parables of Jesus can be interpreted constructively within the contexts of the Gospels in which they are embedded. Yet, in many instances readers can see that tensions arise between a parable and its narrative context. In the parable of the Widow and the Unjust Judge, for example, the Gospel of Luke applies the parable to persistence in prayer to God: if an unjust judge is willing to administer justice to a persistent woman, how much more is the merciful God eager to do so for those who pray? But the chasm between this unjust judge and a gracious God who hears the prayers of the oppressed and acts in loving response to them is an interpretive leap too far. As Barbara Reid notes,

Luke's comparison to fervent prayer "sidetracks the reader" from the parable's core message of relentlessly seeking justice in the face of persistent, systemic injustice, leading many interpreters of the parable to overlook its main point.[20]

Despite the presence of a moral before or after a fable, *mashal*, or parable, the parable itself does not seek to impose a singular response but instead creates a dialogue and invites or challenges its hearers or readers to participate. *Parables, in fact, can be created with and have inherent in their transmission the possibility of having multiple morals, meanings, and applications.* As Theon stated, "It may be possible for one fable to have several conclusions (or morals), if we take a start from each of the matters in the fable" (*Progymnasmata* 4). This aspect of fables and parables is exceedingly important. For example, with this understanding, the seemingly disparate applications of the parable of the Dishonest Steward (Luke 16:1–8a) in 16:8–9, 16:10–12, and 16:13 can be seen as a rhetorical unity instead of evidence of different traditions.[21]

So, Gospel authors also supply diverging perspectives on how the parables they include should be interpreted. The author of each Gospel, even if just supplying a narrative context without explicit commentary, provides a response to and interpretation of every parable. The author's voice enters into a dialogue with the parable—using each one as an aspect of plot and characterization—yet parables, because of the way they function, are not limited to those (canonical) responses: they call for, encourage, and sometimes even demand responses by all those with ears to hear and eyes to see.

Unstated Premises in Parables, Fables, and *Meshalim*

One helpful way to understand how parables, fables, *meshalim*, and visual images often "work" is to identify how their unstated premises engage their audiences. For example, we can state,

> All humans are mortal;
> therefore, Socrates is mortal.

We can easily fill in the missing premise: Socrates is human. Unstated premises in other instances can be more difficult for an audience to supply, but this rhetorical technique heightens its persuasive argument because the audience actively participates in the creation of meaning; it forms a rhetorical bond between audience and speaker. The missing premise is often a common or widely held cultural value, or sometimes a fable or parable can challenge or subvert cultural or other values. The use of a missing premise can lose its effectiveness when audiences have different cultural or other assumptions or views.

Parables and visual images can omit premises of one kind or another, thus leading to ambiguity and multiple meanings. In many instances, such gaps are intentional; ambiguity is an essential element of parables/fables. As C. H. Dodd puts it, a parable leaves "the mind in sufficient doubt about its precise application to tease it into active thought."[22] That aspect of parables can give them tremendous power to affect their hearers and readers in many ways—challenging them to change their attitudes, beliefs, and behaviors. The process provokes divergent responses as interpreters endeavor to understand them, since not every audience member envisions the missing premise in the same way.

Sometimes it is difficult or even impossible to fill in these gaps. Consider this example: "Two people are sitting in a room. They are both silent. Then one of them says, 'Well!' The other does not respond." As Voloshinov/Bakhtin notes, "For us outsiders this entire 'conversation' is utterly incomprehensible."[23] No matter how carefully we analyze the parable's rhetoric or the phonetic, morphological, and semantic elements of its words, we are lost without more context. To understand the parable more fully, we need to know that the two people were tired of winter, it had begun to snow, and it was May. In the case of Jesus's parables, the missing premises sometimes can be similarly difficult or even impossible to decipher and supply.

In other cases, the missing premise can be unintentionally omitted. Modern readers of the Gospels, for instance, are often unaware of many social and cultural assumptions that would be understood by first-century readers. Thus, a key role for interpreters seeking to make the parables relevant for today is to attempt whenever possible to fill in missing premises or gaps with historical, social, and cultural information, such as Howard Thurman's *Jesus and the Disinherited* did. One's interpretative task does not end there, however. Because Jesus's parables *want* something from their hearers or readers, interpreters should then attempt, as Thurman's book also did, to contextualize the parables of Jesus authentically, making them relevant for contemporary society without anachronizing or domesticating Jesus's message. As C. H. Dodd claimed about the pictures these ancient parables create in the minds of today's hearers, parables retain their imaginative and poetic quality:

> They are works of art, and any serious work of art has significance beyond its original occasion....Their teaching may be fruitfully applied and re-applied to all sorts of new situations which were never contemplated at the time when they were spoken. But a just understanding of their original import in relation to a particular situation in the past will put us on right lines in applying them to our new situations.[24]

4

WHAT DO PARABLES WANT?

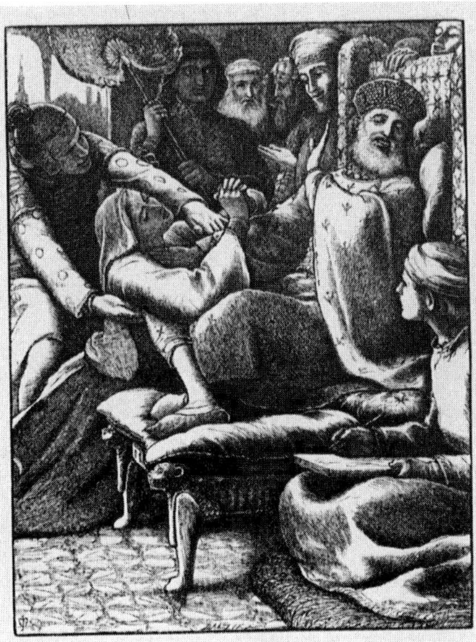

John Everett Millais, *The Unjust Judge and the Importunate Widow*, engraved and printed by the Dalziel Brothers, 1864, New York, Metropolitan Museum of Art, Rogers Fund, 1921.

Diverse interpretations of Jesus's parables over the centuries reflect their inherent and somewhat incongruous complexity, as well as their enigmatic nature. Even systematic analyses of a parable may lead interpreters to find multiple meanings. In addition, all interpreters have subjective, limited perspectives and explicit and implicit presuppositions. On one hand, Jesus's parables are dialogic; they challenge the hearts, minds, and imaginations of their audiences to respond in word and deed. The rhetorical strategies in parables intentionally leave gaps that must be filled in by hearers and readers of parables. On the other hand, there are aspects of parables that first-century hearers would have readily known and understood that are incomprehensible for modern readers who lack knowledge of the parables' first-century contexts. Approaches to ancient texts that incorporate information about common social, cultural, economic, and other patterns in the first-century Mediterranean world can assist interpreters trying to fill in these gaps, but the horizon of historicity continually recedes: because of the limited information available about first-century life in general and historical events in particular, many gaps and ambiguities will remain. As Gerd Theissen appropriately notes, historical scholarship is an ongoing conversation in which no one has the final word.[1] Interpreters can fill in some gaps through a systematic, more comprehensive interdisciplinary approach but must do so in dialogue with other interpreters and modes of interpretations. We are dependent on and in dialogue with other interpreters, past and present, and the pursuit of truth, however elusive "truth" might be, is facilitated by these conversations and debates, especially with those interpreters with whom we may disagree.[2]

TEXTS AND CONTEXTS IN DIALOGUE

In the decades since Thurman's *Jesus and the Disinherited* was published, New Testament scholars have extended (and revised) his insights about the message of Jesus for those with their backs against the wall. William Herzog, for example, showed how the parables of Jesus provide a vision of the kingdom of God, but that they also portray and critique the ruling class's oppression of the disinherited nonelites.[3] Some parables of Jesus in Luke exhibit this dynamic more than others, such as the parables of the Rich Fool (12:16–21), Great Dinner (14:16–24), Rich Man and Lazarus (16:19–31), and Unjust Judge and Importunate Widow (18:2–8). The parables of the Good Samaritan (10:25–37) and Prodigal Son (15:11–32), however, also demonstrate how Jesus's parables want us to respond to such dire situations and need.

In the preindustrial, agrarian society of the first century reflected in the parables of Jesus, nonelites in agricultural production—approximately 90 percent of the population—were at the mercy of elite powerholders. Elites controlled any surplus produced by nonelites, so the vast majority of people lived on a subsistence level. Nonelite "subsistence farmers," for example, had little control over the conditions that governed their lives, and one of their strategies to survive was to form relationships based on reciprocity among those of similar rank and relationships of patronage between those of different socioeconomic levels.[4] Because of their precarious existence, nonelites believed in a "subsistence ethic": everyone was entitled to eke a living out of the resources of the village through reciprocity or patronage. People living on a bare subsistence level thus viewed patronage—where the elites distribute goods to the nonelites—as a moral obligation; people who had resources were expected to help in difficult circumstances.[5]

This "view from below" of Jesus's parables is another aspect they share with (other) ancient fables, and in this case an intertextual analysis of parables and fables helps our understanding of the ways in which the parables of Jesus function in their socioeconomic context. As G. E. M. de Ste. Croix notes, fables in the ancient world were a form of expression "associated particularly"—but not exclusively—with slaves. One of the key elements of the fables of Phaedrus, for example, is how they give voice to the oppressed and include the use of "hidden subversive speech."[6] Phaedrus, a freed slave of Emperor Augustus who used collections of the fables of Aesop (another former slave who probably lived in the sixth century BCE), comments about this characteristic of some parables:

> Now I will explain briefly why the type of thing called fable was invented. The slave, being liable to punishment for any offence, since he dared not say outright what he wished to say, projected his personal sentiments into fables and eluded censure under the guise of jesting with made-up stories. (*The Fables of Phaedrus* 3 prologue 33–37)[7]

Phaedrus claims that fables were invented so slaves could express in a disguised form sentiments that if expressed directly would result in punishment, and many fables certainly reflect perspectives of oppressed, disinherited people (cf. the discussion of African American spirituals in chapter 2).[8] Phaedrus introduces a fable, for example, by noting that the "poor are the most fortunate" in changes in leadership in the state, because such a transition brings no change for the poor except a change in who they call their master or king. The fable itself entails a fearful elderly man in a meadow with his donkey. They were startled by an army of enemies approaching, so the man tells the donkey that they must flee to avoid capture. The donkey, however, was loath to increase his pace, so he asks his owner if the "conqueror" would make him carry two packs instead of just one. When the owner answers no, then the donkey replies that if his burden does not increase, "I care not who is king."[9]

As James Scott points out, interactions between the powerful and the powerless have (1) a "public" or "onstage" transcript—the open, straightforward speech between the dominant and the subordinate in which the subordinate defers to, complies with, and thus reinforces the position of the dominant—and (2) a "hidden" or "offstage" transcript—the subversive criticism of the oppressors by the oppressed that negates the established public order out of hearing of the oppressor. As part of the "weapons of the weak," oppressed people also use covert ways of protesting and subverting the oppressive social order of the elite that has intentional ambiguity. As Scott notes,

> This is a politics of disguise and anonymity that takes place in public view but is designed to have a double meaning or to shield the identity of the actors. Rumor, gossip, *folktales* [emphasis mine], jokes, songs, rituals, codes and euphemisms—a good part of the folk culture of subordinate groups—fits this description.[10]

Similarly, Jesus uses hidden subversive speech in various sayings and parables, with perhaps the most misunderstood ambiguous, subversive response being, "Then give to the emperor the things that are the emperor's" (Luke 20:25). This saying is a "hidden transcript" of nonelite resistance against an extractive taxation system that transferred wealth from the majority of people in the Roman Empire to the ruling elites. Since the denarius coin that Jesus referenced would have been inscribed, "Tiberius Caesar, son of the divine Augustus," Jesus most likely is saying for disinherited people with ears to hear, "Give that blasphemous coin back to that blasphemous emperor."[11]

Jesus's parables, like other fables from disinherited people, portray situations intimately familiar to the rural poor, including images of the systems of oppression that held them in bondage and kept them in poverty.[12]

> Jesus was an impoverished first-century Jewish artisan who was a member of a politically, militarily, and economically oppressed minority and who spoke prophetic words of judgment against the oppressors of his people. His parables and other teachings focus extensively on issues of money and power, including condemnations of the wealthy elite because of their oppression of the poor. Such socio-economic contexts thus are essential for understanding numerous aspects of the parables of Jesus.[13]

How should wealthy elites live? Jesus in Luke declares, for example, that they no longer should be "lovers of money" (16:14) driven by greed. Instead, Jesus demands that they operate with vertical generalized reciprocity—a redistribution from the advantaged to the disadvantaged that expects nothing in return.[14] Since God showers humankind with vertical generalized reciprocity, humankind should follow God's lead in their relationships with each other (e.g., 11:11–14).[15] Jesus advises the elite, for example, not to engage merely in reciprocity among equals by inviting their friends, relatives, and rich neighbors to their feasts, but instead to invite the poor, crippled, lame, and blind. The elites' concern for money is linked to their lack of concern for human beings, and this connection between riches and unrighteousness can only be broken through vertical generalized reciprocity (14:12–14; cf. 16:9, 19–31).

THURMAN'S UNDERSTANDING OF THE PRODIGAL SON AND GOOD SAMARITAN PARABLES

As Thurman's *Jesus and the Disinherited* demonstrates, Jesus lived with his "back against the wall," and his message was primarily aimed toward those who, like him, were dispossessed and disinherited, coupled with a prophetic judgment of the dominant, the powerful, the rich. Jesus's message affirmed the inherent worth of the disinherited as children of God, the necessity of the love-ethic to pervade all relationships, and the power of love to create community in the midst of and even over against the forces of evil.

That message is still relevant to the disinherited and the oppressed of every age, and Dodd's contention that the pictures these ancient parables create in the minds of today's hearers "may be fruitfully applied and re-applied to all sorts of new situations" is certainly correct. Jesus spoke his parables in his own historical context as a disinherited, oppressed first-century Jew, and his powerful critique of the wealthy can be found in those parables. His love-ethic leading to restoration of community that is rooted in his Jewish faith is also ever present, and we see it clearly in such parables as the Prodigal Son and the Good Samaritan.

The parables of the Prodigal Son and Good Samaritan are foundational to Thurman's life and thought, fundamental to his understanding of the religion of Jesus, and, in our continuing search for common ground, exemplify a path toward *community* with God and our fellow human beings. These two parables are found in the Gospel of Luke, which was written by someone in a very different socioeconomic position than Jesus. In one sense, then, Luke's Gospel contains the kernels of the book that Thurman contemplated writing about "Jesus and the inherited"—the message of Jesus for the advantaged, powerful, and rich.[16] Although Luke certainly includes Jesus's message for the disinherited, a major focus in Luke is the warning this message has for the inherited.

In that light, part 3 and part 4 of this book have a twofold task, with the teacher's guide introducing a third. First is the attempt to understand as best as possible the parables of the

Prodigal Son (part 3) and Good Samaritan (part 4) in their first-century historical, social, and cultural contexts. Second, using insights from Howard Thurman, these explorations will seek to contextualize the parables of Jesus authentically, making them relevant for contemporary society without anachronizing or domesticating his message. Third, the teacher's guide will use visual art to, as Thurman envisioned, endeavor to raise spiritual consciousness and deepen community. The ultimate goal is, by exploring what these parables want and using the insights of Howard Thurman, to continue the quest for common ground, for community, for, to paraphrase his words, "a friendly world of friendly human beings."

Part III

Two Sons and Their Father

A Parable about Us

5

LISTENING FOR THE WHISPER OF GOD

"THOU HAST TO CHURN THE MILK"

Albrecht Dürer, *The Prodigal Son amid the Swine*, 1496; New York, Metropolitan Museum of Art, Robert Lehman Collection, 1975.

But Jesus spake in a parable, and he said:
A certain man had two sons.
Jesus didn't give this man a name,
But his name is God Almighty.
And Jesus didn't call these sons by name,
But ev'ry young man,
Ev'rywhere,
Is one of these two sons.

James Weldon Johnson[1]

The parable of the Prodigal Son fascinates readers because they tend to identify with one of the two sons in the parable, while assuming that the father symbolizes God.[2] Engagement with the parable is also generated by the parable's compelling human themes—sibling rivalries; conflicts between older and younger generations; dynamics of justice, love, and mercy; loss and restoration of community and family; and the implications these have for human and human and divine relationships. In addition, the parable provides minimal explanations of why characters act and speak the way they do, and these ambiguities add to the fascination with these three characters. The parable is also famously open-ended: readers are not told, for example, whether the older brother is ultimately convinced by his father and joins the celebration of his brother's return. What few readers recognize, however, is that the younger son's perspective is also ambiguous: it leaves unsettled whether the son "comes to his senses" and concocts an insincere plan to manipulate his father or whether he actually repents.

Interpretation of the Prodigal Son parable is made more difficult because of its context in Luke as the third and final of the three "Lost and Found" parables in Luke 15 (Lost Sheep, Lost Coin, and Lost Son). This placement encourages readers to believe that the prodigal son repents, thus supplying the Gospel's preferred answer to the question about the son's motives and sincerity that the parable itself leaves ambiguous.

THE GENERAL CONTEXT IN LUKE

In the narrative of Luke, the parables of the Lost Sheep, Lost Coin, and Prodigal Son are directed to the same audience: "Pharisees and scribes" who grumble that Jesus "welcomes sinners and eats with them" (15:1–2). Jesus responds to this complaint by addressing to "them this parable." Repetitive words and themes link the three parables, emphasizing their common concerns: repentance (15:7, 10, 18)—although a lost sheep or coin is not capable of repentance, and the prodigal son may not be either—and communal joy over the lost being found (15:6–7, 9–10, 23–24, 32).

The parable of the Prodigal Son builds upon the positive reactions to the celebrations in the first two parables, drawing a contrast between those celebrations and the celebration of the prodigal son's return that his brother refuses to join. In its Lukan setting, the parable also illuminates characters in the larger narrative. The younger brother demands his inheritance, leaves home, squanders his inheritance in dissolute living, ends up hungry and tending swine, and then returns to his father; he represents those sinners coming to hear Jesus's message. The elder son, who never left home but becomes estranged from his father when he refuses to join the celebration and feast for his wayward brother, represents the opponents of Jesus who grumble over Jesus welcoming sinners and eating with them. The father symbolizes God, who receives sinners with love and entreats others to celebrate their return. The blessings of God also belong to those who "grumble," but they must understand that God shows grace to all people.[3] Thus, in Luke, all three "Lost" parables defend Jesus's ministry to "tax collectors and sinners" and declare that his opponents should join the celebration over the lost being found.

This "first reading" of the parable in Luke's Gospel dominated interpretations of the Prodigal Son parable in the intervening centuries, with the focus being the repentance of the prodigal son and the love, forgiveness, and compassion of the father. A close reading of the parable itself, however, may suggest that the love, forgiveness, and compassion of the father does not depend on the repentance of the prodigal and that the parable ultimately may be urging its readers to identify with the father. This recognition opens the possibility that Jesus's message was even more striking than Luke's "one sinner who repents" message (15:7, 10). Its open-endedness, however, also has significant implications for what is needed to establish and maintain community.

The parable can be divided into three scenes. The first focuses on the younger son who leaves home and then returns. The second focuses on the father's reception of the younger son; the third focuses on the older brother—his initial reaction and whether he will respond positively to his father's entreaties. However, the parable revolves around the father and his words and actions of love.[4]

THE DEPARTURE (LUKE 15:11–13A)

The Prodigal Son is the longest of Jesus's parables, but it still only offers information essential for the story, compressing and omitting details, and leaving tantalizing gaps and ambiguities. The three main characters are a father and his two sons, and the most important unanswered question remaining at the conclusion of the parable is whether the two sons will reconcile as brothers and as sons with their father.

The parable opens with the expectation that tension will arise between the two sons in their relationships with the father, echoing older-younger brother dynamics from the Hebrew Bible (e.g., Esau and Jacob, Joseph and his brothers). Because of the Hebrew Bible contexts of younger brothers being favored (e.g., Abel over Cain, Jacob over Esau), readers initially would be inclined to prefer the younger son. Jesus's parables, however, sometimes subvert expectations.

The first word spoken by a character in the parable is the younger son addressing his father with a respectful title ("Father"), but what follows is surprising. He demands ("give me") his inheritance, one that he, the parable makes clear, should not receive ("will belong") until after his father's death.

Contrary to the advice in Sirach 33:20, 22 that warns against prematurely giving an inheritance to one's children, the father agrees—without rebuke or protest—and divides the property "between them."[5] Although the son's demand may not reach the shocking "You're dead to me" level that some commentators suggest—but note that the father divides the *bios* (life) between the two sons in 15:12—it still is disrespectful to the father, rejects family ties, and thus is indeed seen as irresponsible if not offensive to the audience.[6] The presence of the admonition in Sirach against this practice indicates, however, that such arrangements were not unheard of; rules tend to be introduced when people are acting in ways that make a rule seem necessary. Yet it would have been offensive to most (if not all) first-century readers that the younger son transforms his inheritance into disposable income, especially while his father is alive.[7]

Although the first sentence of the parable evokes the biblical theme of the favored younger son who succeeds (as do Jacob and Joseph), the second sentence brings to mind the biblical theme of rebellious sons, who usually are not successful (cf. Eli's two sons Hophni and Phinehas in 1 Sam 1:22–36; 4:1–11). The parable's audience is surprised both by the son's demand and the father's acquiescence. The son is rebellious, the father is foolish, and the son compounds his rebellion by leaving his family and departing for a distant land.

Insights from Howard Thurman

Thurman does not refer to the parable of the Prodigal Son as extensively as he does the Good Samaritan, but it is just as foundational to his life and thought, including his search for redemptive experiences, common ground, and community. Elizabeth Yates's biography of Thurman illustrates this quest with an experience from Thurman's time as a graduate student. During the summers, he served as assistant pastor at a church in Roanoke, Virginia, and part of his duties included leading vacation bible school. One summer, a problematic youth disrupted the programs, and Thurman several times had to exclude the boy from taking part. As a result, when invited to the last day of the program, the boy refused to attend.

> Howard urged [the boy] to join in with the others.
>
> "But you put me out," the boy said. It was a fact he could not get beyond.
>
> Looking at him, yearning to see him take his place in the group, Howard felt that he had somehow failed the boy....
>
> What was involved, Howard asked himself, in the loss of an opportunity to relate meaningfully to another human being? Even if the boy might sometime feel sorry, that would not redeem the time that had been lost now. When the prodigal son returned to his father—and Jesus had ended his story at the point where his hearers could pick it up—did he wrestle till he died with the problem of how he could ever redeem the time interval during which his relationship with his father had been ruptured? The wheel of time could

> not be made to turn back, *but any experience could be made redemptive.*[8]

Over the course of Thurman's career, the parable of the Prodigal Son is an implicitly recurring emphasis in his thought, illustrated best, perhaps, in the ways he felt compelled to explore how to create redemptive experiences and to work to build common ground and community. In this quest, Thurman's distinctive interpretations of this parable play a key role.[9]

In a sermon on the Prodigal Son preached at Fellowship Church on September 23, 1951, Thurman argued that the first point in this "simple story" is that "God is like the father, and that anybody may be like the prodigal son, and that anybody may be like the older brother. We all stand in that relationship, the family relationship with God, and you are lost if you are out of primary fellowship with God, whatever else you may have."[10] The focus, then, is on the nature of fellowship, of *community*, with God and with other human beings.

We can postulate that Thurman's discussions of the Prodigal Son parable reflect in part his own seeking of "symbolic fathers," both physical and spiritual,[11] but an undeniably crucial context for Thurman's understanding of the parable stems from a story he relates many times over the course of his career. His grandmother—probably seventeen years old when the Civil War started—was enslaved on a plantation in north Florida, just outside of Tallahassee. Twice a year the owner of that plantation permitted one of the workers he enslaved to preach to the other enslaved people, and in every sermon, no matter the subject, the preacher would end the sermon by looking intently at all in the congregation, dramatically assuring them that they in reality were "not slaves condemned forever to do their master's will," and then forcefully declaring, "You are God's children!" When Thurman told this story in a 1972 sermon, "Footprints of the Disinherited," he noted that this message might seem "simple and almost so naïve now" but

> we have forgotten that the only true basis for a sense of security...is the awareness that you are precious in the sight of God, that you are of worth, and that your worth is not derived from anything that you do, any-

thing that you have, anything that you know....Now this is the contribution that the religion of Jesus makes to mankind.[12]

Thurman does not explicitly mention the Prodigal Son or Good Samaritan parable in this sermon. Yet the sermon reflects central components of his interpretations of both parables: Jesus proclaims the "God of the whisper in the heart" (e.g., when the prodigal "comes to himself") which does not result in a "sectarian, parochial religious experience" that excludes others. Instead, Jesus declares that God is the father of all people and that every single human being is our sibling. This relationship, Jesus asserts, transcends all barriers and establishes a "universal brotherhood" and, in fact, a "universal morality": "So it means that all the time we've got to keep broadening, widening our religious experience in order that we might be able to support brotherhood as defined in this new and tremendous way of the Master. And this is why he talks so much about love."[13]

For Thurman, the key question in all the Lost parables in Luke 15—sheep, coin, and son—is "What is God like?" He explores this question in his sermons about these three parables "to deal with the meaning of the relationship of the human spirit to God, which is, after all, the fundamental point of all religion."[14]

DISSOLUTE LIVING (LUKE 15:13B–16)

Jesus quickly gets to the point: the younger son "squanders his property in dissolute living" (15:13b), but these words are ambiguous, in contrast with the older son's more explicit accusation about his younger brother and "prostitutes" in 15:30. At the very least, readers learn that the son was an irresponsible spendthrift who lived extravagantly.

The younger son's fortunes decline relentlessly, first because of his bad choices and then because of a severe famine. He therefore hires himself to—literally, "clings to"—a citizen of the country to which he had traveled, and he works feeding pigs. According to Mosaic law, pigs are unclean (e.g., Lev 11:7–8). His status thus declines from being the son of a wealthy landowner to being a laborer on another (Gentile) person's property, performing a task that no Jewish person should perform. His degradation and desperation are accentuated by his desire to eat the food he was assigned to give the pigs.[15] The younger son leaving his family and country resulted in a demoralizing lack of community and, therefore, he lacks a web of relationships on which to depend, as the devastating description of his plight concludes: "and *no one* [emphatic in Greek] gave him anything."

The contrast between the father who had given him everything he demanded and the citizens of a distant country who gave him nothing in his great need is striking. Generosity and hospitality are key concerns of this parable; the son's plight is a result of his own foolish mistakes, ruinous misfortune, and a lack of hospitality from others. The younger son's downward spiral has reached the lowest socioeconomic level: that of an "expendable"—who lived at or below subsistence level, where mere survival was a constant struggle, and death was usually close at hand.

Insights from Howard Thurman

Thurman marvels about the "consummate touch of genius" of Jesus the storyteller, of the profundity, complexity, and nuance of these "simple stories" that elucidate Jesus's vision of the nature of God, the divine/human relationship, and the nature of community with God and other human beings.

Thurman avoids painting too negative an image of the prodigal son, which, though it tones down the prodigal's offensive behavior, humanizes him and makes him more relatable. In his 1951 sermon on the prodigal son, for example, Thurman says the son wants to "go away" so he can "try [his] wings."[16] In Thurman's 1954 sermon, he elaborates even more: the younger son asked for his inheritance because he had plans, travelling to a far country, "to get as far away from any controlling influence as possible."[17] Thurman continues by saying that the prodigal also enjoyed himself and, of course, "found friends everywhere" who would help him spend his money. In the 1951 sermon, Thurman observes that their friendship lasted "only to the last coin" (cf. Petronius, *Satyricon* 80.9), but in 1954, in which the sermon takes a slightly different tack, he posits that after the money ran out, the friends might have tried to help, offering the prodigal a place to stay "for a week or so," which the prodigal politely declined.

The prodigal son's hunger then drove him to hire himself out as a keeper of pigs, a devastating blow to his pride and self-respect. This desperate action shows Thurman the evil times that this "sensitive son of Israel" faced and what he was forced to do to survive. The young man was "beyond the reach of the climate that sustained him," and in his desperation, he reached the low point of his young life.

THE PRODIGAL "COMES TO HIMSELF" (LUKE 15:17–19)

The son's utter destitution leads to another major transition in the story: the son "came to himself" (15:17) and devises a plan to try to reverse his downward trajectory. The ambiguous "came to himself" could be interpreted in at least two ways. One option—suggested by the parable's placement as the third parable in the Lost and Found trilogy—is that the son repents.[18] Another option is that "came to himself" means that he "came to his senses," since Luke's preferred term for repentance is not used in the parable.[19] In this view, the starving son remains a shrewd, self-centered person who concocts a plan that might convince his father to at least house and feed him as a hired hand. The fact that the son rehearses his speech—parables are usually economical in their use of words—reinforces the idea that the son was trying to manipulate his father. In addition, as Amy-Jill Levine argues, "biblically literate" hearers of the parable recognize the biblical patterns encouraging them to identify with the younger son (e.g., Jacob versus Esau) and also suspect that the prodigal does not repent but "connivingly" concocts a plan so that he will no longer be hungry (cf. Exod 10:16; Luke 12:17; 16:3; 18:4–5).[20] As George Hubbard put it in his 1906 book, *The Teachings of Jesus in Parables*,

> But mark, there is no repentance for his sin, no upspringing of love for his injured father, no true regret for his

own ingratitude. Those who make this an example of true repentance read something onto the story that Jesus never put there. It is simply the desire of a hungry man for something to eat.[21]

The planned speech includes the confession that the son had sinned against God and against his father,[22] had destroyed kinship ties,[23] and therefore no longer deserved to be called a son, but it closes with a suggested resolution: that the son be treated as a hired hand. However, such interior monologues in Luke's parables—compare the Rich Fool (12:16–21) and the Unjust Judge (18:4–5)—often reflect the inner turmoil of characters who "tend to be *un*-heroic, requiring correction."[24] Even telling his father his preferred solution about being treated as a hired hand is presumptuous. So, although the context of Luke leads readers to interpret "came to himself" as repentance, the parable itself is ambiguous about whether the son repents or merely realizes how foolishly he had acted against his own self-interest.

INSIGHTS FROM HOWARD THURMAN

> [The son] never "leaves" in the sense that no matter where he goes—given the proper understanding and relationship of son towards father—he will be in his father's house "at all times and in all places."
>
> Archimandrite Vasileios[25]

THE THREE "LOST" PARABLES: THE BEGINNING OF COMMUNITY

Thurman uses the Lost Sheep, Lost Coin, and Prodigal Son parables as a starting point to explain how we move from isolation to community in his October 24, 1954, sermon, "Jesus Speaks of Salvation."[26] These three parables show Jesus's understanding of what is involved in salvation: a restoring of community. The lost coin, for example, was "out of its function" and restored. The sheep became lost "while doing the most natural thing for a sheep," eating and following the grass, not realizing that he had left the other sheep behind. Once the shepherd realizes the sheep is lost, he sets out to find it, and rejoices when the sheep is found intact: "And if the community were intact, then no fundamental harm could come to it. So the shepherd was very happy."[27]

Thurman then dwells extensively on the Prodigal Son parable, adding details, filling gaps, providing his perspective. Here again Thurman humanizes the prodigal, downplaying the negative actions that helped create his dire situation. The focus now is on his desperation, the degradation of his spirit that led to "a stirring down at the bottom of his being." Jesus described it as a "coming to himself" that said, "You are lost. You are out of contact with your family. You are out of community. Why don't you go home?"

Thurman's retelling of the parable diverges from the text, not just filling in gaps but tweaking it to make his theological point. The son creates a speech, but in Thurman's retelling it includes the explicit desire for community: "I know I have made a mistake. I know I have done this and this and this and I'm sorry. I don't want anything, but I just want to be near so that I can have a sense of community again. No demands. Just to be near so that little by little I can warm my spirit with the love of my father. That's all I want." And Thurman ends his version of the parable there since his hearers "know the rest of the story." The older brother is left outside, because Thurman wants to get to the heart of the parable as he understands it. The three Lost parables illustrate the fundamental primary relationship that individual human spirits have with God that nothing can destroy:

> I wonder if you believe that. God loves the sinner, not merely after the sinner repents. No. But God loves the sinner before he repents, and it is the moving intensity of the love of God [without which] we rot and die. We can't stand being cut off, being isolated, and that is what Jesus is saying. The lost man is the isolated man, the man who is out of touch with the things that feed and sustain his life.[28]

Thurman captures the essential element of the parable: the father (God) loves the son (the sinner) even before he repents. Most importantly, human beings are lost if they are not aware of their sense of community with God. The good news is that God and God's love are relentlessly seeking us, and in response to God, "something deep within you will begin to move," and you will begin to open doors deep within you until at last you will find "that which you have had all along." As Thurman concludes about the prodigal son, "When he came to himself, he went to his father and when he looked in his father's face, he realized that in his father's face, he saw that he, the boy, had never left home."[29]

The Prodigal Discovers Who He Really Is

In his sermons and other writings Thurman often argues for a deeper spiritual meaning of when the son came to himself and envisions it as an exemplar for the spiritual journey and necessity of "coming home" for every human being; his mysticism-guided vision means that human beings discover God within themselves and, in doing so, realize who they really are.

In his autobiography *With Head and Heart*, for example, Thurman relates a conversation he had in Colombo, Ceylon (now Sri Lanka), in 1935 with a Buddhist man who was troubled about the influence of Christianity on Buddhist students. The man observed that such students tended not to become Christians but abandoned their Buddhist faith and became "spiritual drifters." Thurman responded by using the parable of the Prodigal Son as an illustration of "the inward journey":[30]

> It seems to me that Christian education has succeeded if it makes a man an authentic Christian, or it may make him a better and more completely devout Buddhist. For I believe that Jesus reveals to a man the meaning of what he is in root and essence already. When the prodigal son came to himself, he came to his father.

What this means for Thurman is that one's religious faith and experience should keep a person "grounded" and able to "come to himself whole, in an inclusive and integrated manner, one that would not be possible without this spiritual orientation."[31]

The Prodigal Discovers That God Is within Him

Thurman's book *The Creative Encounter* provides the necessary context for what Thurman envisions occurring when the prodigal son "comes to himself." For Thurman, the central fact in religious experience "is the awareness of meeting God." Sometimes this awareness is the sense of "Presence"; other experiences can be better described as encounters and some even as confrontations. However it is described, the core of the experience is being "exposed to direct knowledge of ultimate meaning, *ne plus ultra* being, in which all that the individual is, becomes clear as immediate and often distinct revelation."[32] It is in this context that the prodigal's experience must be understood as Thurman put it in his 1951 sermon on the Prodigal Son:

> "When [the prodigal] came to himself," he came to his father....When I...come to the very center, the very core of myself, then I come face to face with God. That God is, God is within me. That he is the very point of my being and existence....That there is that of man which is God. Not a reflection of God. Not some staggering accent of God, but that which *is* God.[33]

One of the ways that Thurman explained the presence of God within "the inward parts of the human spirit and the human heart" was to borrow an image from Hinduism: "the butter is in the milk," and "Thou has to churn the milk...if thou desirest to taste the butter."[34] God is found within human beings who have to cultivate awareness of God within them, and one necessary path was to "limit one's intake," to slow down and focus on important things amid the multitude of distractions in our hectic and harried lives, since there can be a "striking relationship between the inner and the outer" aspects of our lives. Instead, we must churn the milk of our inner selves so we may taste the butter.[35]

Here we see why Thurman continually insists it is critical for human beings to look inward, to search their hearts, to reflect, meditate, and contemplate in quietness, to center down in stillness, to become aware of the whisper in our hearts that the hustle and bustle of everyday life drowns out, and to gain clarity and assurance. Thurman's meditations and his use of the fine arts to heighten spiritual consciousness show how his mystical vision impacted his life and thought. This vision led him to consider not only our perception of ourselves but the mystery and wonder of our relatedness.

A 1958 sermon, "Mood to Linger," sheds further light on what this relatedness involves. Thurman argues that, especially in a world filled with distractions, human beings need to cultivate the mood to linger, to meditate in solitude and quietness, and to reflect on life's ultimate questions and the direction of our lives in response. In this sermon, Thurman uses the mystic Meister Eckhart to illustrate how one must cultivate living out of one's "inmost center," which requires time, dedication, stillness, and meditation. In these times of centering, human beings can have a primary and basic encounter with God.[36]

Although the Prodigal Son is the scriptural text for the "Mood to Linger" sermon, Thurman only refers to it once, briefly noting that when the son "came to himself," he "came to his father" to explain his understanding of what that means for him: "That which is deepest in me is always reaching out to that which is deepest in life. And when these two come together then I have a sense of being whole, and this can only be done when in many, many ways and in many aspects of our lives, we cultivate quiet, we study ways in which we can reduce the traffic of our days."[37]

Thurman shares in this sermon illustrations of how this experience can be cultivated and what is accomplished when it is. When Thurman was a student in Rochester, New York, he walked down busy Main Street many times with traffic all around him, but one night he walked home after midnight after teaching an evening Bible study. There were no streetcars and no traffic, and as Thurman walked in the quiet, he thought he heard rushing water. He realized that he had been hearing that rumbling for a while, but it took some time in the quiet for him to realize what it was. He mentioned this event to one of his professors the next day, and the professor confirmed that Thurman had indeed heard the sound of water—what the professor said was part of the Erie Canal—a sound that was impossible to hear during daylight hours with the sounds of people and traffic.[38] Similarly, Thurman observes, we must cultivate quietness in our own lives "to pick up sounds" from the deepest part of ourselves.

Only when we learn how to be quiet, to center down in the stillness, can what is deepest inside us move into our awareness. One of Thurman's students, Walter Pahnke, a deep-sea diver, wrote a paper about an experience he had "at the bottom of the Caribbean Sea." After diving down, Pahnke sat on a large coral and observed what was around him. Soon he realized that he was in the middle of what appeared to be a flower garden that had not been there when he first arrived. But as soon as he moved, every flower disappeared. He could not see or experience those flowers when he was swimming around; it was only in the stillness, when he blended in with the life around him, that the beautiful garden appeared. Thurman concludes that these experiences—and that of the prodigal son's "coming to himself"—are characteristic of human life.[39]

The fact that God exists within every human being has profound implications. Once the prodigal son had opened that interior door of himself to God, everything changed. And so it should change for all human beings in their communion with God, their fellowship with other human beings, and their social actions. As Thurman says in his 1951 Prodigal Son sermon, having that communion with God allows human beings "to find a tool, to fashion a tool that will be vehicular for them, that will be the means by which they can provide an escalator from the churning spirit that is within them to the external world."[40]

It is never too late to "come to oneself," to end the self-imposed estrangement from God. As Thurman observes,

> For the moment, deep within you, you come to yourself, you find waiting there your father, who can take your limitations, all of the broken manifestations of your day's or year's journey and brood over them with his infinite wisdom, tenderness, and knowledge of the whole meaning of existence and place at your disposal that which will make you his son. That is yours. That's mine. And I'm grateful to God that it is so. Grateful, grateful to God that I'm his son, and he's my father.[41]

The Prodigal Son and "The Sound of the Genuine"

Thurman discusses the presence of the divine within each human being perhaps most famously in the appropriately and most likely deliberately ambiguous characterization of the "sound of the genuine." The sound of the genuine was a theme Thurman addressed extensively beginning at least in 1935 and continuing throughout his career.

To introduce the idea of seeking the sound of the genuine within oneself, Thurman often quotes from or summarizes the story found in Catherine Cate Coblentz's *The Blue Cat of Castle Town* in which the blue cat learned the "song of the river" and to "Sing your own song. Sing well." Eventually the cat spent most of his time in the different houses of Castle Town, and he "sang and sang to everyone who would listen." As a result, people began to speak less of "gold and power and more and more they talked of beauty and peace and content[ment]."[42] Thurman used this "simple story" to urge his hearers and readers to seek to hear, then listen to, and finally to follow the sound of the genuine in themselves and to listen for the sound of the genuine in others.[43]

In a May 1, 1977, sermon, for example, Thurman begins by saying that "there is something in every man that waits and listens for the sound of the genuine in himself."[44] The genuine is at work in God's creation, and human beings become "out of touch" when they do not listen to the sound of the genuine within them. In fact, Thurman declares, the awareness of our own reality is connected to the awareness of God in us. Without that awareness, we "stumble in the darkness." Although Thurman does not refer directly to the Prodigal Son parable here, that is the plight of the prodigal; he was stumbling in the darkness and out of touch. Interestingly, Thurman also does not cite the parable of the Good Samaritan explicitly in this sermon either, but he does tell the story of the compassionate Samaritan from his youth, the anonymous man in the Daytona railway station who paid for Thurman's trunk to be transported to Jacksonville so Thurman could attend high school (see chapter 7). Thus, in this sermon, we also see the implication of the sound of the genuine within us that leads to the actions of the compassionate

Samaritan—listening to the sound of the genuine creates community. Thurman says,

> There is something in every man that waits and listens for the sound of the genuine within himself. There is something in every man that waits and listens for the sound of the genuine in another man. Listen and you might hear the whisper of God that comes through the sound of the genuine.[45]

When we listen for and respond to the sound of the genuine in another human being, we are ascribing to them the same sense of infinite worth that we (should) believe that we have. This sound of the genuine is another aspect of our common consciousness, and here the power of imagination takes root and gives us the ability to put ourselves truly in the place of another human being.[46]

The Relationship between the "Inner" and the "Outer"

In his 1951 Prodigal Son sermon, Thurman notes in passing how sometimes there appears to be a relationship between one's external environment and what is reflected inside of us, although he warns his congregation not to "push that too far." The famine throughout the land, for example, is reflected not only in the prodigal's physical hunger but also in his internal spiritual famine: "the clue to the outer is the inner. The famine that the boy experienced in the far country, he was already experiencing in his own heart. It's very simple."[47] Such perspectives are reflected, of course, in much visual art portraying the destitution of the prodigal when he "comes to himself" among the swine, such as the engraving by Albrecht Dürer, where the dilapidation of the architecture in the etching mirrors the son's physical and spiritual destitution.

THERE MUST BE COMMUNITY

The implications of the Prodigal Son parable relate to Thurman's understanding of the "profoundest dimension" of religious experience: "the finding of man by God and the finding of God by man. This is the inner witness." Individuals bring all their errors, imperfections, and blindness to this encounter, including the scar tissue developed along the way, but this encounter allows them to see themselves from another point of view, with life's baggage laid aside, and standing without hindrance or "possible protection from the countenance of the Other." It is like a birth or rebirth of a new self, and a new center is found in this creative encounter.[48]

Prayer is one of the vehicles for an encounter with the divine when individuals use prayer to enter into the "temple of quiet" within their own spirits and foster the activity of their spirit within themselves. When people prepare themselves in this way, the initiative moves from their own hands into God's because God is "a seeking and beseeching God," as, Thurman argues, the parables of the Lost Sheep, Lost Coin, and Prodigal Son demonstrate.[49] We become aware of God in the "hunger of our hearts," and it is through the discipline of prayer we learn God's will and God's purposes in the world.[50] And what is disclosed through prayer? "The moving finger of God in human history points ever in the same direction. There must be community."[51]

6

THERE MUST BE COMMUNITY, OR, A FATHER'S LOVE, A BROTHER'S ANGER

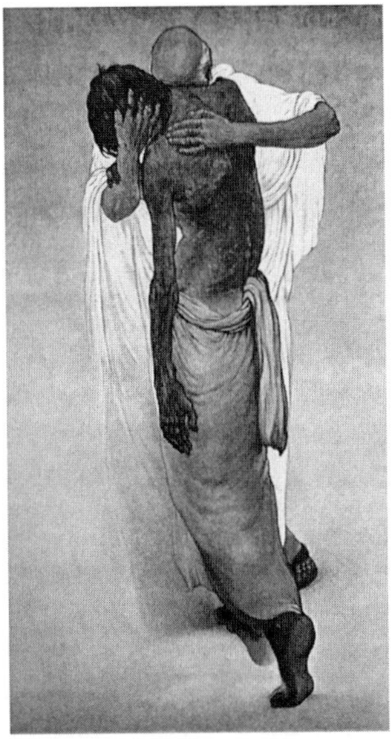

Frank Wesley, *Forgiving Father*. Hiroshima Girls School, Japan. Used with permission of the family of Frank Wesley. http://www.frankwesleyart.com/main_page.htm.

What saves the younger son is his comprehension that he is his Father's son....

The father is noble in his love. He cares not about himself but is more concerned with saving someone else, his child. This is the purpose of his life and the most worthy part of his being. He cares not what the world will say about him, nor that he might lose his prestige, nor that as a father, he might seem a failure.

Archimandrite Vasileios[1]

RETURN AND RECEPTION (LUKE 15:20–24)

Although this section of the parable narrates the interaction between the younger son and the father, the focus of the story shifts to the father, emphasizing his words and actions. The son's urgency is clear: After coming to himself, he leaves immediately because of his desperate need. Likewise, the father's hopeful anticipation is clear: The same Greek word "far" (*makran*) creates a poetic parallelism between the son traveling to a "far country" and his father seeing him return from "far off." That the father saw his son while the son was still far off seems to imply that he had been watching for his son, and the following verses show the father's eagerness to welcome him back as a full, valued member of the family. The parable reveals the father's motivation for his words and deeds—*compassion*—which is crucial to the parable's major point and builds upon earlier scenes in Luke:

- When Jesus met the burial procession of a widow's only son: "When the Lord saw her, he had *compassion* on her" (Luke 7:13).
- In the parable of the Good Samaritan, the Samaritan came upon the wounded man: "and when he saw him, he was moved with *compassion*" (Luke 10:33 author's translation).
- In the parable of the Prodigal Son: "his father saw him and was filled with *compassion*" (Luke 15:20).

Compassion connects all three of these stories that in some way revolve around a "death," one literal, one potential, and one metaphorical. The first story involves Jesus bringing a dead man back to life. The Good Samaritan involves someone helping a "half-dead" man recover. The father in the Prodigal Son describes his son's departure/absence as death and his return as being "alive again." In the parables of the Good Samaritan and Prodigal Son, then, the Samaritan and the father model the compassion that Jesus shows for others, the compassion of God that Jesus himself embodies, and the compassion that Jesus commands his followers to have for all human beings, ranging from closer relationships (parents and children) to more difficult ones (people considered strangers and even enemies).[2]

The description of the father's actions includes a series of staccato-like verbs in Greek that demonstrate his love, compassion, and welcome: He *ran*, *put his arms around him* ("fell on his neck" like Esau did with his returning estranged brother Jacob in Gen 33:4), and *kissed* him (the verb signifies continuous action, kissing him over and over). The son begins his prepared speech, uttering it word for word like he had practiced, but his father interrupts (the son does not get to say, "treat me like one of your hired hands"). Strikingly, the father speaks not to his son at this point but to his slaves and gives orders that demonstrate the joyful restoration of the son into the family with orders to clothe his son in the best robe, put a ring on his finger and sandals on his feet, and kill the fatted calf so they could celebrate the son's return. Here and elsewhere, the father is still in command of the "property," and, whether for the slaves, the son, or the readers, the father includes an explanation for his commands: "this son of mine" was dead/lost and now is again alive/found (15:24).

The father responds to what had been a public embarrassment of him by his son with a public demonstration of his son's restoration to a place of honor within the family. Many interpreters argue that the son's restoration would have been witnessed publicly;[3] if accurate, then the extravagant loving actions of the father are accentuated even more. The starving son who would have gladly eaten the pods he was feeding pigs in a distant country is now feasting on a fatted calf back home with his father and, presumably, many others who were called to celebrate, which parallels the celebration of the shepherd with his friends and neighbors after finding the lost sheep (15:6) and the woman with her friends and neighbors after finding the lost coin (15:9). When the son "came to himself" (15:17), he noted that his father's hired hands had "bread enough and to spare," so his father's response goes well beyond the son's hopes. No one in the distant country had given him anything; in contrast, his father gives him everything.

Interpreters often overstress how shocking some of the father's actions are. It is important to realize, however, that "unusual behavior is not unrealistic behavior."[4] Yes, the father's actions are extravagant, as are the Good Samaritan's (see part 4). At the very least, the father was doting, indulgent, and permissive, with words and actions that appear uncharacteristic, unexpected, and unusual, but there is enough evidence to suggest that the father's response is indeed plausible.[5]

Missing from this parable is any mention of punishment, recrimination, or retribution. The father welcomes his son back joyfully, no questions asked, and no demands made. Although some interpreters argue that such a reception should be expected of a loving father, that case is hard to make. Other interpreters point out that in ancient societies, both Gentile and Jewish, the most common view was that the son should have been punished. See, for example, the possible punishment for a "stubborn and rebellious" son who is "a glutton and a drunkard" in Deuteronomy 21:18–21. Numerous ancient texts, both Jewish and Greco-Roman, relate how rebellious sons should be treated, as well as the expectations, and sometimes laws, that sons support their parents during their later years.[6] On the other hand, numerous Jewish texts reflect the loving, compassionate God who yearns for the return of God's wayward children and who welcomes them with loving, forgiving arms (cf. Jer 31:18–20; *Peskita Rabbati* 184b–185a).[7]

This parable is a Jewish portrait of a loving, compassionate father. Some interpretations draw a direct parallel between this human father and God. That the son states that he had sinned "against heaven" (God) and his father, however, complicates a simple allegorized reading of the parable that equates the father with God. That comparison is even more difficult when the human father is seen as imperfect—even foolish. But the conclusion remains that love, compassion, and restoration of community are of paramount concern, even in a flawed, dysfunctional family, which, perhaps, can be of comfort and inspiration to other flawed and sometimes dysfunctional communities who "come to themselves" and (re)discover a loving and compassionate God. So, in the end, the likelihood is that this parable is a Jewish story about how God deals with God's children.

In the context in which Luke places this parable—the third and final of the Lost and Found parables in Luke 15—the story should be read as one of repentance and celebration of that repentance (see Luke 15:1–2, 6–7, 9–10, 32). The parable itself, however, is more ambiguous, and, in fact, suggests something even more radical about the father's love and compassion: the same extravagant loving actions should be offered whether the son was "truly" repentant or whether he was still trying to manipulate his father. As we have seen, Jesus in Luke argues that vertical generalized reciprocity—the advantaged giving to the disadvantaged without expecting anything in return—is the means by which wealthy people can enter heaven (e.g., Luke 14:12–14; cf. 16:14, 19–31). This parable, then, may offer a similar message: assistance to those in need should be given even to those who may be—or appear to be—undeserving.[8]

The urgency of celebrating the son's return is highlighted by the statement that "they began to celebrate" immediately after the father finishes his speech in 15:21–24. Yet readers will remember how the parable began in 15:11: the father had *two* sons; the story is not yet complete.

Insights from Howard Thurman

The Prodigal Son and the Jewish Love-Ethic

Thurman interprets the parable of the Prodigal Son in the context of the religion of Jesus. Jesus saw God everywhere, caring about everything—the lilies of the field, the grass on the hillside, the number of hairs on a human head. Thurman says, "This was Jesus's religion. God the shepherd, seeking the lost sheep. God the heartbroken father waiting for the return of his willful and recalcitrant son; God the be-all and the end-all of life."[9] Thurman's interpretation also highlights the importance of the "inner life" of reflection, meditation, and prayer; Jesus was constantly aware of the ever-present God, yet he, during the demands of his ministry, had to detach himself, withdraw, pray, and spend time alone with God.

Jesus experienced God's love, a love that breaks any sense of isolation and assures us that we are never cut off from community: "there is something that happens to you when you become aware of the fact of love as it is moving towards you, that releases you, that frees you, that makes it possible for you to relax your inner sense" and to share everything, including doubts, limitations, and defects, with "quiet confidence."[10] Jesus thus uses the parable of the Prodigal Son to illustrate how the love of God operates, and Thurman dwells on it extensively in his 1956 sermon, "The Love of God." A key aspect, in addition to the forgiveness of the prodigal, is that the prodigal had to "purify himself of the self-judgment" that resulted from his violation of the loving relationship between him and his father. How the son could "work out his salvation" in his father's household sheds light on the love of God and religious experience. In the presence of God, we learn that God's love transcends any individual particularities or limitations. God deals with the core of our being: "In quietness, in prayer, it is here that I become aware of the meaning of the love of God." Thurman also notes that one can experience God in other modes, such as in the natural world, and "it is in the moment when I as a human being am able to experience this sense of being completely and totally understood...is the ultimate immunity against isolation. This is the only bulwark against the devastation of affliction." Understood by God, accepted at the core of our being, we thus have a radical confirmation of community. We are at our core sustained, confirmed, and in community with God.[11]

Therefore, the foundation of community is built on the loving actions of God. But a human response to the whisper of God in our hearts is also required. Even though the parable itself is ambiguous about whether the younger son truly repents and whether the older son ultimately reconciles with his father and brother, the desired outcomes are clear for both, and the restoration of community is dependent on those responses of repentance.

The Restoration of Community through Love

In his 1951 Prodigal Son sermon, Thurman does not dwell on the return of the son, briefly noting that the father did not give his son the chance to finish his speech and in "that swirling moment of heightened ecstasy," in multiple ways showed his love for his returning son. Like the shepherd searching for the lost sheep, the woman looking for the lost coin, and the father running out to meet his returning son, God desires to restore human beings to the fellowship and community to which they belong. As Thurman concludes in his 1953 sermon on the Lost Sheep, "That is how God is, if we let him."[12]

Thurman's mystic vision is that individuals sense or experience the love of God at the "center" of themselves in ways that transcend their own virtues and vices. They feel at home in this existence, but then hunt for clues to this experience in God's creation and seek to cultivate the same experience with their fellow human beings—experiences with God and others that meet the deepest need of their lives.[13] They care about other human beings regardless of personalities or divisive aspects and deal with others in concrete rather than abstract ways. This care for others begins with sensitivity, awareness, openness, and acceptance.[14]

To say that one loves "humanity" is meaningless; one must endeavor to understand and love individual human beings. One cannot truly love "the hungry" or "the homeless" without loving and caring for in some concrete ways individuals who are hungry or homeless. Part of caring for other human beings involves serious attempts to understand their context and situation. Understanding other people's contexts involves more than just acknowledging their predicament at a particular point in time; this effort also seeks to become aware of their potential. To truly love people involves, as Thurman liked to put it, meeting people where they are and dealing with them as if they were where they should be.[15]

Thurman returns to this essential point in his 1957 "Religion of Jesus" lecture series. He summarizes this process of restoration, reconciliation, and community in his "Lost Sheep and the Lost Coin" lecture in that series, which also discusses the Prodigal Son parable. Thurman returns to his theme that the religion of Jesus is "God-centered," and, therefore, that "fundamental to life is the divine purpose, and the divine purpose is that there shall be increasingly, in all creation, community, a sense of ingatheredness, a sense of wholeness, a sense of integration." Human beings, created in the image of God, desire and hunger for this sense of wholeness, of community, and we are lost without it, isolated. Unlike the lost sheep or lost coin, the prodigal son deliberately separated himself from his community. But then,

> Jesus says that [the prodigal] came to himself. He discovered that which was deepest in him, that which he most fundamentally desired over all else...[and that] was precisely what God wanted. I am my father's son, and my father is my father. When he became aware of this, salvation became operative.[16]

This recognition is possible, Thurman argues, because as God's children, "there is within us the mark of his creation." That "mark" is a "sensitive, palpitating, quivering divine dimension of us that is always seeking to align, to get us into harmony, to complete the cycle between [us] and God." The movement toward God, then—such as the prodigal's "coming to himself and the father"—is a "shared initiative"; it can occur because of the "persistent pull of God" leading us to reestablish community with God and, consequently, with others. "God can never be happy," in fact, until all human beings live in community with God and with all other "living things." The sense of community that emerges, the desire to reestablish a lost harmony, involves the awareness, acceptance, and active work toward a collective destiny:

> For better or for worse, God and I, God and you, are bound together, and I cannot be what it is that I must be if between you and me, between you and God, there is no community....God cannot be happy in his heaven if any man is in hell. Therefore, I must work out my salvation by seeking in every way to further communion between myself and all living things and myself and God.[17]

Thus, Thurman argues, we must actively work toward meeting the needs of other human beings, to restore, build, and maintain community. This inner awareness of the presence of God and of all humankind as children of God leads us to work diligently on behalf of our brothers and sisters.

Another explanation of the critical components of such

reconciliation is found in Thurman's 1963 book *Disciplines of the Spirit*. Reconciliation, he argues, is intrinsically connected to religious experience, where human beings encounter the divine in their very core, and this awareness permits them to recognize their true self and sets in motion the process of their integration, their coming to wholeness: "The experience of the prodigal son is underscored in the religious experience of the race—when he came to himself, he came to his father's house and dwelling place." This experience of God brings peace, healing, and redemption, so human beings must keep open the path that allows their father and them to "have free and easy access to each other." The ethical imperative of this religious experience extends to reconciling with other human beings, as Jesus makes clear in his command to reconcile conflicts with other human beings before "offering your gift at the altar" (Matt 5:23–24).[18] This observation leads to the issue of the older brother's rejection of his wayward brother.

THE OLDER BROTHER, THE FATHER, AND THE PRODIGAL (LUKE 15:25–32)

> The parable's genius is its capacity to create identification with each character, which means that we experience the story from conflicting perspectives.
>
> Paul Duke[19]

Parables are often evocative, suggestive, and surprising. We now find, for example, that the older son had not yet been invited to the festivities and, in fact, did not even know that his brother had returned: this "elder" (*presbyteros*) heard "music and dancing" and had to be informed what was happening by a slave boy (*pais*).

Surely this omission adds to readers' sympathy for the older brother, since he, once again, seems slighted. The older son so far appears to be hardworking and loyal to his father (e.g., he was "in the field" working when his wayward brother returned), and now his share of the inheritance is a real concern: the return of the younger son and the celebration with a fatted calf meant that his own share of the inheritance was already being used to support the younger son. Understandably, then, the older son becomes angry at such apparent unfairness, and the father, like he did with the younger son, goes out to meet him. Yet there are key differences; unlike with the younger son, the father does not run out to him, put his arms around him, or kiss him.

In addition to the father's differing initial reactions to his sons, the contrast between the father's compassion for the younger son and the older son's anger begins a reversal; once the older son appears on the stage, the parable begins to build a negative portrait of him. His refusal to enter the house and to celebrate his brother's return insults his father, and the father comes outside to plead with him; the Greek word *plead* can mean to "invite," "exhort," "encourage," or "comfort." Then the older son disrespectfully addresses his father without a title, states that he had "never disobeyed" his father's commands (although, if true, he is rejecting his father's entreaties now), and begins a litany of (exaggerated) complaints. He stresses his servitude to his father and complains about how his father had treated him. He accuses his father of favoritism and attacks his younger brother by refusing any familial relationship with him, referring to him not as "my brother" but pejoratively as "this son of yours" (15:30), and stressing and perhaps exaggerating the younger son's failings. His claim that the younger son "devoured your living with prostitutes" might be questioned. How did the older son know that information, and is it true?

One option argued by Callie Callon is that Luke, in telling a story that featured prodigality, could avail himself of one of the stereotypical features of prodigality common in Greco-Roman comedy: "expending one's patrimony on love interests, particularly prostitutes." The purpose of the older son's accusations is to defame his brother in a way that might also seem humorous to the intended audience. Another common feature in such comedies is the restoration of the prodigal through his father's forgiveness, which coheres with the Prodigal Son's plot as well.[20]

By this point in the parable, the older brother is not a reliable source of information. How long had such resentment and anger been festering inside him? Perhaps it was not just since his younger brother's departure but "for all these years" (15:29). Because of this negative characterization, readers might wonder whether the older son who remained at home and was seemingly the dutiful son also had been estranged from his father. At the very least, he is estranged at this stage, and, once again, the father responds with love and compassion.

The ambiguities of the parable leave its readers to consider the alternatives. How much of a point does the older son have? Had the father, as many fathers in the Hebrew Bible, favored the younger son and neglected the older son? The fact that the father had overlooked inviting the older son to the banquet lends some credence to the son's complaints—another insult the older son could add to his list—and the father now attempts to placate his son for his earlier neglect by saying "all that is mine is yours." Yet, on the positive side, the father responds to his son's "never" (15:29) with an argument of "always" (15:31).

The parable thus is a study of contrasts: the contrast between the younger son who leaves home and the older son who remains sets the stage for the contrast between the father and the older son upon the younger son's return. The father who sees his younger son returning from far off contrasts with the older brother who remains in the field unaware. The father welcomes the younger son back with joyous, open arms, but the older son refuses to recognize his brother as family. The older son proves that he is no more loving than the younger son.[21] The father, though, shows similar tenderness with his older son. Even after the older son rebukes him and refuses to address him respectfully as "father," the father chooses to address his older son with an affectionate title (15:31, *teknon*: "son" or even "my dear child"). The father does not directly address most of the complaints listed by the older son, but he focuses again on the restoration of family community. Similar to how he responded to the younger son, the father offers no recrimination or rebuke beyond one gentle reminder of familial ties: He stresses to the older son that the younger son was "this *brother* of *yours*" (15:32; cf. the older brother's "this *son* of *yours*" in 15:30) and that "it was necessary" to receive the lost son back into the family with celebration.

The parable begins, "There was a man who had two sons," and it dramatically demonstrates how much the man loved his two sons, showed generosity to both, met them where they were, and, in the process, betrayed little or no concern for his property or the ways in which he had been slighted/insulted. The unanswered question of the parable is whether those two sons will reconcile as brothers and be truly in communion with their father. The parable similarly extends an invitation to its readers, offering love, compassion, reconciliation, and a joyfully celebrating community. By doing so, however, the parable also demands an answer from its readers to the open-ended question concerning their own unresolved conflicts: Will they accept the invitation in whatever form it comes in their lives and act accordingly?

Insights from Howard Thurman

What Is God Like? The Restoration of Community with God

Thurman stresses that God the father looks for both sons, goes out to meet them, and demonstrates his love and compassion for them. The good news is that the younger son is restored to the community; whether the older son is restored remains unanswered by the parable, leaving the answer in the hands of those who hear this compelling story.

Thurman observes that anyone can be a prodigal returning—or needing to return—home to their father, and anyone can be the elder brother whom the father entreats to rejoin the family and join the celebration, being restored to community in a way similar to the younger brother. Younger brothers should "come to themselves" and return to fellowship with God and their fellow human beings. Older brothers should not only join in celebration of the restoration of community for others but in doing so also end their self-estrangement from God and others and be restored to full community.[22]

Thurman does not dwell long on the older brother in the parable. His 1951 Prodigal Son sermon, for example, briefly characterizes the older son's words and actions, similarly portraying him in the best light possible just as he does the younger son. Although his "rumbling was so significant" that the father comes out to speak with him, Thurman emphasizes the very human nature of the older son's anger and resentment against the special treatment the younger son received considering the older son's commitment to staying and working. In Thurman's retelling, the father emphasizes the empathy and "sensitiveness" to what his brother's return meant: "He was lost and now is found." In essence, Thurman notes, the older son, without ever leaving home, was "out of fellowship nevertheless." He, like his brother, was estranged from his father—symbolizing being out of fellowship with God the father—and, like his brother, needs to be restored into fellowship—symbolizing the need to be restored into fellowship with God and with other human beings.[23]

What Is God Like? The Restoration of Human Community

In a 1951 sermon, Thurman connects how experiencing the spirit of God in quietness, in meditation, or as the prodigal son did in his abject despair, leads also to a sense of relatedness with God and with other human beings and, therefore, our commitments to other children of God:

> No one of us can live unto himself no matter how hard he tries. We are so deeply involved in each other and in others that often it is difficult to determine where we begin and the other leaves off. And perhaps in the quietness we may sense the mystery and the wonder and the magic of our relatedness, and in that relatedness become aware, each after the pattern of his own sensitiveness, of the emergence in our midst of the living spirit of the living God in whom we live and move and have our being.[24]

Thurman's plea to his congregation is that what they discover in their own quiet reflection will not only inform them but also spread—partly through their own efforts—to all humankind.

In contrast, Thurman stresses that the lack of fellowship with God negatively impacts our relationships with other human beings and results in the further loss of the community that sustains us. Therefore, as noted in chapter 5, Thurman's interpretations of the Prodigal Son parable focus primarily on the question, "What is God like?" Doing so leads to questions about what that means for human endeavors: What are the implications of God's love for human beings? Answering the question "What is God like?" inherently leads to Jesus's call to act as God our loving parent does (e.g., "to be merciful, just as [God] your Father is merciful"; Luke 6:36). In that way, human beings can act to restore and preserve *community*, a fundamental issue of "salvation" for Thurman.

In his sermon "The Love of God," Thurman speaks about how the experience of God's creative love leads to extending similar love to our fellow human beings:

> It seems to me that this points up an important thing about the love of God. In the religious experience, the individual finds fulfilled what he has glimpsed in his other experiences of love: namely, that in the presence of his God he becomes aware of being dealt with totally. Whether he is a good person or a bad person, he is being dealt with at a point beyond all that is limiting, and all that is creative, in him. He is dealt with at the core of his being, and at that core he is touched and released. With insight, with wisdom, with patience, with courage, with devotion, with commitment, he can now deal with the facts of his own life; and he will seek to introduce all these qualities into his relationships with his fellows.[25]

Just as the "inner" relates to the "outer" (see chapter 5), the establishment of community with God necessitates (re)actions that directly affect how one lives and how one relates with other human beings. These insights thus begin to illustrate how Thurman envisions the fact that the religion of Jesus insists on the inherent connection between one's inner spiritual life and one's resulting actions. It is only after inner transformation has begun that the focus may begin to include how to translate and implement those ultimate realities into concrete, practical actions in one's daily life. In his sermons in particular, Thurman seeks to instruct but more importantly guide, inspire, and work to create a communal experience of God's all-embracing presence. It is then and only then that his sermons, as do the parables of Jesus, challenge his listeners. How does Thurman's perspective, then, connect with what the parable of the Prodigal Son "wants?"

CONCLUSION: ACTING LIKE GOD

> Thurman's lifelong project of creating real human relations between people...[involved] being able to see what was God in us, ridding ourselves of the spiritual obstacles that made such a vision impossible, and then transmitting that knowledge into movements to transform and redeem the social world—this was his lifelong vision.
>
> Paul Harvey[26]

In January 1949, Thurman preached a sermon, "Love Your Enemy," that he later published in his book *The Growing Edge*.[27] Thurman begins the sermon by quoting Jesus in Matthew 5:44–45: "Love your enemies that you may become children of your Father who is in heaven, who causeth the sun to shine on the just and unjust, who causeth the rains to fall on the good and the bad." Thurman deduces that God expects human beings to be like God. Thurman's insight of the "amazing concept" that the "creative mind and spirit of God *dares* to assume that it is within the range of possibility for human life that men [and women] shall become and shall behave and perform like God"[28] is similar in some ways to how Henri Nouwen approaches the Prodigal Son parable. Nouwen interprets the parable as reflecting developments in a spiritual journey of homecoming, affirmation, and reconciliation, with creative insights about Rembrandt's *The Return of the Prodigal Son* (1667–1669), on Rembrandt's many other representations of the parable, Rembrandt's own life, and Nouwen's own stages-in-life.[29]

Nouwen concludes that he (like Rembrandt) identified with all three characters in the parable at different stages of his life.[30] The first phase was the experience of being like the younger son, a story that reflects "the history of our salvation": sin, repentance, and return to God.[31] The second phase was identifying as the elder son and determining whether to join the celebration welcoming home one's repentant brothers and sisters.[32] The third and final phase came when a friend, Sue Mosteller, opened Nouwen's eyes to the main message of the Prodigal Son parable: "Whether you are the younger son or the elder son, you have to realize that you are called to become the father." As a result, Nouwen came to understand that the message of the parable was to claim one's "true vocation": "Look at the father in the painting and you will know who you are called to be." Becoming a repentant child is but one step on the path to becoming the welcoming father.[33]

Thurman's observations are also similar to those of Hieromonk Gregorios, who argues that God created human beings in the image of God to make them communicants of divine love. Thus, God adorned human beings "with life, logos, wisdom, and all the divine qualities" so they "would aspire to the corresponding divine good." Human beings, created in the image of God, should aspire to transition from the *image* of God to the *likeness* of God, which occurs through love: "This is the state to which the Saints aspire in order to resemble God: the state of perfect love."[34]

The father shows such love to both his sons, and the parable demands that human beings act toward their fellow human beings—their brothers and sisters—with similar welcoming love and compassion.

Such love and compassion are also the pathway that leads to Thurman's interpretations of the parable of the Good Samaritan, especially since the introduction to the parable in Luke 10:25–28 includes the "love commands" to love God and to love one's neighbor as oneself. In his sermon "Love Your Enemy," for instance, Thurman states that this difficult process of loving one's enemy must begin with loving oneself. The key to loving oneself is the recognition that as a child of God one is of infinite worth. As Thurman declares, every human being can say, "I have in myself a basic confidence that there is in me that which is holy and divine and beautiful." That status applies to every human being; everyone is a child of God, of infinite worth, and worthy of respect—even those people who are "enemies." Jesus demonstrated this love, for example, with tax collectors such as Zacchaeus (Luke 19:1–10).[35] Such an outlook also explains why Jesus picked a Samaritan as the hero of compassion and mercy to emulate ("Go and do likewise"; Luke 10:37). It also explains why, like the parable of the Prodigal Son, the parable of the Good Samaritan was so foundational in Thurman's life and work.

Part IV

The Compassionate Samaritan

An Apostle of Sensitiveness

7

TRAUMA ON THE ROAD TO JERICHO

James B. Janknegt, *Portrait of YOU as the Good Samaritan*, http://www.bcartfarm.com/.

> If as a people we have made a covenant with God, then we have an ethic by which God is measuring our relationship with him. We are truly God's children to the extent that we are brothers and sisters to one another, and we are less God's children when we no longer treat others as neighbors, when we exploit them because we do not see them as images of God and as our brothers and sisters. We have here a true theological logic that derives from God and is imparted to humanity and the church. It is called the "sacrament of unity," the unity of humankind with God and of human beings with one another.
>
> Oscar Romero[1]

> This parable is annoying, for it will not let us avert our eyes.
>
> Klyne Snodgrass[2]

One of Jesus's most beloved parables relates how a Samaritan responded to a traumatized man (the Greek word for *wounds* in Luke 10:34 is *traumata*) after two other men had "averted their eyes" and ignored the man in need. The most common English title for this parable, the Good Samaritan, does not accurately capture the parable's essence. The title normally used in German, the Compassionate Samaritan or Merciful Samaritan (*Der Barmherzige Samariter*) is more accurate.[3] Whatever title is used, as Emerson Powery notes, the parable "is a story about the kind of community Jesus envisions for the world."[4]

GENERAL CONTEXT IN LUKE

As with the Prodigal Son parable, Luke provides the interpretation of the Good Samaritan partly through the context in which the story is embedded in the overall narrative. The parable occurs in the lengthy travel narrative section, which begins when Jesus "set his face to go to Jerusalem" (9:51). This circuitous journey covering approximately eighty-five miles takes almost ten Lukan chapters, ending when Jesus enters the Jerusalem temple (19:45).[5]

The Good Samaritan is the first of approximately twenty-five parables in Jesus's journey to Jerusalem. Readers are first introduced to Samaritans shortly after Jesus begins his journey when a village of Samaritans do not "receive" Jesus because he was going to Jerusalem. This lack of hospitality creates a negative impression of Samaritans with readers, but the parable of the Good Samaritan works to reverse this impression, instead portraying a Samaritan as an example of faith-in-action.

The parable of the Good Samaritan arises in response to a lawyer who "stood up to test Jesus" and asks, "What must I do to inherit eternal life?" This question by a recognized religious authority is an unfriendly challenge to Jesus's person and authority. Note, for example, the Greek word that is translated as "test" in 10:25 is the same word used in Luke 4:2, where Jesus was "tempted" (tested) by the devil. The lawyer is "testing" Jesus in a way similar to the devil, which adds to the lawyer's negative portrait.

Jesus responds to the lawyer's challenge with his own questions aimed at the lawyer's area of expertise: "What is written in the law? What do you read there?" (10:26). The lawyer's first response (10:27) combines Deuteronomy 6:5, part of the Shema (Deut 6:4–6) and Leviticus 19:18, part of the Holiness Code (Lev

17—26), where people are enjoined to be holy because God is holy (19:2). He replies that one must love God fully—with all of one's heart, soul, and strength (Luke 10:27 adds "mind," as does Mark 12:30 but not Matt 22:37)—and to love one's neighbor as oneself. These two love commands are foundational to Judaism; the Shema, for example, is recited twice a day (Deut 6:7, cf. m. Berakoth 1:1–4). They also form the foundation on which Jesus's message is built. The love for God comes from the innermost center of one's being, and the love of one's neighbor results from one's love for God. Since the lawyer already knew the answer to his question, people witnessing this encounter between Jesus and the lawyer now would realize, like the readers already know, that the lawyer was just trying to trap Jesus; the lawyer thus looks foolish.

Jesus responds that the lawyer answered correctly and says, "Do this, and you will live" (cf. Lev 18:5). The focus is on action, not just knowledge, because *knowing* what is right is not the same as—and much easier than—*doing* what is right.

After Jesus affirms the lawyer's answer, the lawyer attempts to "justify himself" (10:29) by asking, "And who is my neighbor?" George Hubbard makes a striking observation about this question. He argues that even asking the question, "Who is my neighbor?"

> betrays the unneighborly spirit....The truly neighborly soul will never stay to ask, "Who is my neighbor?" Such souls are too busy seizing every opportunity to manifest the neighborly spirit, to perform some neighborly kindness....Whenever you find yourself asking, "Who is my neighbor?" you may be sure that something is wrong in your own heart....What you need is not information, but transformation.[6]

In response to this question, Jesus tells the story about a merciful Samaritan and concludes it with a question that the lawyer is forced to respond to with an answer he does not want to give (10:37, where he avoids saying the word *Samaritan*). The parable illustrates not just who proved to be a neighbor but what it means to love God and one's neighbor. In answering the question this way, Jesus stands firmly within the rabbinic tradition of *meshalim* (parables/fables) of Torah/scripture being a central element of the meaning and application of the story.[7]

THE GOOD SAMARITAN PARABLE: THE TRAUMA AND LACK OF RESPONSE (10:30–32)

The parable begins with a "certain human being" (*anthropos tis*) going down the road from Jerusalem to Jericho. Who is this person, and what is he like? We know the ethnicity of three characters in the parable—priest, Levite, Samaritan—and at least one detail about two others—robbers and innkeeper—but not this human being; this person could be anybody (rich or poor, Jew or Gentile, etc.). Although hearers may envision a male Jew, the parable itself leaves ethnicity ambiguous, and that ambiguity, which remains throughout the entire parable, is essential to the greater impact of the story.

Jericho is an oasis in a wilderness about eighteen miles northeast of Jerusalem, but the elevation drops over 3,300 feet as you descend from Jerusalem to Jericho. The road between Jerusalem and Jericho was known for being dangerous and desolate. Josephus describes it as "a wild, desert terrain" (*Jewish War* 4.474), and Strabo notes that Pompey's army destroyed "strongholds of brigands" near Jericho (*Geography* 16.2.41). Josephus also observes that bandits—the same term used in the parable—were common (*War* 2.8.4).

Although the parable only mentions clothing being stolen, most interpreters assume that the robbers took whatever else the person had with him. The theft of clothing also removes aspects that would make the person's cultural identity, wealth, and social status evident, as well as depriving the person of dignity and honor, so passersby would have little clue as to the wounded, naked, and humiliated person's status.[8]

The beating is an act of gratuitous violence since the bandits had already stripped the man and brutalized him afterward. The parable provides no reason for this senseless act of violence. In addition, the term "half dead" is ambiguous. Is this man unconscious and looking like a corpse or injured so badly that his life was in peril and he needed help to survive? The term as it is used in Strabo, Diodorus, and Siculus means the latter, but that intertextual context is not definitive for its use in Luke. Readers may identify with this anonymous person who is brutalized on the way to Jericho. This man is the only one who appears in every scene, and, although a completely silent and passive character, is the starting point for answering the lawyer's question, "Who is my neighbor?"

"By chance" the first person on the scene is a priest going down toward Jericho, who sees the injured man and (deliberately) "passed by on the other side" (10:31). The surprising term "by chance" suggests a random event, not something directed or controlled by God, and the parable thus remarkably does not assure its readers of a positive ending.[9] The parable gives no (explicit) reason for why the priest did not stop to assist the wounded person, but interpreters usually offer the following suggestions:

Fear of robbers. Ancient literature records instances where one bandit pretends to have been attacked, and then his fellow bandits would rob people who stopped to help. If this is the case, the priest was focusing on his own well-being, not the well-being of the wounded man,[10] and, to be sure, passing by on the other side does not prevent potential robbers from attacking him.

Ritual purity. This interpretation, perhaps the most common, argues that since the beaten man was "half dead," the priest passed by because of potential issues of ritual purity. According to Leviticus 21:1–2, for example, a priest may not "defile" himself for the dead except for his nearest relatives. Any Israelite who touches a corpse is unclean for seven days (Num 5:2; 19:11–13). This hypothesis runs into several problems, however. In the first place "half dead" is ambiguous. The wounded person may only require some sort of "medical" assistance. Even if the priest assumed the person was dead or would possibly die, later Jewish texts, such as the Mishnah and Talmud, not only give a priest permission to bury a neglected corpse (e.g., m. Nazir 7.1; b. Nazir 43b), but he is required to do so. A corpse needing burial takes priority over religious purity (cf. the pious Tobit in Tobit 2:1–8). The parable also seems to imply that the priest did not even bother to verify whether the "half dead" man was alive. Our best evidence suggests that the consensus among first-century Jews, including priests and Levites, is that saving a life is much more important than any potential issues of purity.

Heartlessness. The priest simply did not care enough to stop and help. As the parable will later suggest, the priest's lack of compassion was the problem. The priest "saw him" and "passed by on the other side." This verse speaks volumes through its economy of words.

The next character appearing in the story is a Levite who "likewise" came upon the wounded man, saw him, and "passed by the other side" (10:32).[11] We are given fewer details about the Levite (e.g., we do not know which direction he was traveling), but again, like the priest, we are not told why this man passed by and did not help. The priest and Levite are examples of what the parable does not want its hearers to emulate.

Insights from Howard Thurman

Identifying with the Traumatized Man

Thurman's reflections on this parable do not focus extensively on the traumatized man, but he clearly identified with the man, reflecting on his own personal and religious experiences. Thurman, for example, felt deeply indebted to a mysterious Good Samaritan whose act of generosity was a seminal event during a decisive moment of trauma in Thurman's early life. He even dedicates his autobiography *To the stranger in the railroad station in Daytona Beach who restored my broken dream sixty-five years ago.* This stranger functions as a paradigmatic Good Samaritan whose benevolent actions, Thurman believes, totally changed his life.[12]

Thurman relates this incident many times, but the most detailed version is found in a March 26, 1965, broadcast of *Face to Face* on NBC:

> I remember many, many years ago, when I was just beginning to enter high school, and I was going from the little town in which I lived to a larger city where I would have the opportunity for attending a high school, because, at this period in my state, which is the state of Florida, there were only two public schools in

the entire state that were open to me....When I went to check my trunk, I was told by...a rather unsympathetic ticket agent, "You will have to send this to Jacksonville by railway express." I only had enough money to buy a ticket and, perhaps, a dollar and fifteen or twenty cents left over, and when he said this, I found that the cost of expressing the trunk was about a dollar and seventy-five cents. So my dreams were gone, and I sat on the steps of the railway station, weeping, as we say, crying my eyes out.

And then, when I opened my eyes so that I could see just a little, I saw two rather large feet just in front of mine. And then my eyes crawled all the way up the full height of this man whom I had never seen before.... He said to me, "Boy, what are you crying about?" And then I told him. And he said, "How much does it cost?" I said, "Oh, about a dollar seventy-five cents." And then he said, "Come with me. If you're trying to get out of this town, to get an education for yourself, the least I can do is to help you." So, he paid for the express charges on the trunk. When the receipt was given to him, he handed it to me, and then he wished me well, turned, disappeared out of the door, walking down the railway track.

I had never seen him before, nor have I seen him since, but because of what he did that particular morning, it was possible for me to begin the long pilgrimage which has led to all of the variety of experiences of my life.

We are all indebted to people whose names we do not know, whose faces sometimes we are not able to see....I am not myself alone, but I am a part of all the life that breathes through me and through which I breathe. We are all of us indebted to a vast host by which we are surrounded.[13]

Both the number of times Thurman recounts this story and the dedication of his autobiography to his own Good Samaritan make clear just how important the event was to him. Thurman's perspective, one that identifies with the wounded man in the parable, answers the question posed by the lawyer in Luke 10:29, "And who is my neighbor?": the person in need. Thurman repeatedly stresses just how critical these acts of mercy can be. The act by Thurman's Good Samaritan allowed him to begin his own "pilgrimage," and he connects this indebtedness and gratitude to the vast host who are connected as part of all life. This excerpt thus reflects his perspective on the unity of all life, our connection and interdependence, and our responsibility to "pay it forward."

The Love Commands

> The word was Love,
> Hate is the last great fortress of the weak....
> Thou must not make division.
> Thy mind, heart, soul, and strength must ever search
> To find the way by which the road
> To all men's need of thee must go.
> This is the Highway of the Lord.
>
> Howard Thurman[14]

In a brief meditation ("Thou Shalt Love") in his 1953 book *Meditations of the Heart*, Thurman gives his perspective on the love commands in Luke 10:27. First, love God, which means having a deep sense of relatedness to God, a relationship that gives "energy and power" to deal with the mysteries and struggles of life. Second, love one's neighbor, in which one's relatedness to God inspires creating and maintaining the relatedness with others "that will feed the springs of kindness and sympathy." Third, love yourself, which means to love yourself "with detachment," in ways that are pleasing to God, and with a "self-regard" that makes us "whole and clean in [our] own sight and in the sight of God."[15] This latter aspect—loving oneself—is often overlooked by commentators but not missed by Thurman. To love one's neighbor as oneself by necessity means that you should love yourself, and an essential foundation of truly loving oneself is the recognition that you are a child of God and that God loves you. Loving oneself leads to what appears to be selfish love, but it is instead loving one's neighbor as if the neighbor were you.

The importance Thurman attributes to having, as a child

of God, the capability to love oneself as the foundation for loving others can be seen in the informal eulogy he delivered in a sermon at Fellowship Church on February 1, 1948, after the murder of Mahatma Gandhi.[16] Thurman reflects on his meeting with Gandhi twelve years before, recalling how Gandhi spoke about the difficulties of his campaign of *satyagraha*—"truth force," or nonviolent confrontation. One of the difficulties that the "masses [of people] in India were unable to sustain so creative an ideal for a time interval of sufficient duration to be effective [is] because they do not have the vitality." They lacked vitality because of their poverty and hunger, but a key component also was "a lack of self respect." The lack of self-respect was not primarily due to the oppressive rule of the British empire, Gandhi said; it was "because of untouchability in Hindus," which, among other things, "harms the soul of human beings who look with contempt on other human beings."[17] Every human being is a child of God deserving of respect.

In this instance, Thurman notes, the methods and goals of Jesus and Gandhi are similar. Just as Jesus believed that the only path to true liberation from Rome was by loving the Romans and other "enemies" such as the Samaritans, Gandhi felt similarly about the British. Both, strikingly, were confident that "God could not be defeated...despite all of the present indications to the contrary."[18]

Another similarity between Jesus and Gandhi is in their message to the disinherited and the ways that message has profound implications for society. Here again, for Thurman, the Good Samaritan parable plays a foundational role. For example, Thurman makes a passing reference to the parable in the third lecture of his important 1937 six-part lecture series, "The Significance of Jesus," in which Thurman's more radical views during the 1930s, including socioeconomic concerns, reflect clearly the mind and heart of Jesus of Nazareth in the applications of the two love commands fundamental to Judaism—love of God and neighbor. Thurman notes that these love commands are in "fundamental opposition" to the "grounds of security" to which human beings in the modern world cling, "for it demands the willingness to renounce all personal claims" to private property.[19] Citing sayings of Jesus about not being able to serve God and mammon and seeking God's kingdom instead of worrying about food, drink, or clothes, Thurman concludes, "Ultimately, experimenting with this principle will lead an individual to put himself squarely against the possession of all personal property and to recognize it as a thing making for evil in the world and to work in all ways for legislation and for public opinion that would make private property impossible." In such a society, the security of each individual is guaranteed by all individuals: "It seems to me, therefore, that the Christian in the modern world is called upon to work out a scheme of political organization and machinery designed for the managing of social life on this basis."[20]

This message foreshadows Martin Luther King Jr.'s famous sermon at Riverside Church in New York City on April 4, 1967, in which he said that not only should individuals be Good Samaritans but that the "whole Jericho Road must be transformed so that men and women will not be constantly beaten and robbed as they make their journey on life's highway."[21] Thurman explains what this means for each person: it involves changing the world into a place where the lack of assistance from the priest and Levite are seen as abnormal, and the

> story of the Good Samaritan would be normal, rather than unique as life is now lived. As a matter of fact it would not be necessary for a man to accumulate possessions. In the second place, a man's life with regard to everybody would be covered with a wide series of simply gratuitous deeds of unasked-for kindness.[22]

Society should thus be structured in a way in which everyone's needs are met, and accumulation of wealth is unnecessary. The love commands, Thurman argues, should be put into practice in every area of our lives.

Modernizing, Humanizing, and Applying the Parable

A common response to Jesus's parables is the tendency to domesticate them, to cloak just how demanding and radical they are. In that way, interpreters can consciously or unconsciously salve their consciences and still believe that they are following the teachings of Jesus. A famous example of such domestication is the common misconception that when Jesus says that the wealthy entering the kingdom of God is as likely as a camel going through an eye of a (sewing) needle (Matt 19:24; Mark 10:25; Luke 18:25), he was referring to a mythical gate in Jerusalem through which it was difficult for a camel to pass. In reality, no evidence indicates that the saying refers to a gate, including a particular gate in Jerusalem; it is most likely a fiction that arose during the Middle Ages.[23]

In many ways, Thurman's domestications of the Good Samaritan—like his interpretations of the Prodigal Son—modernize the parable (post-Holocaust) to make it more relatable, understandable, and, in different ways, challenging. His 1951 Good Samaritan sermon, for example, humanizes characters in the parable in subtle but thought-provoking ways, letting his hearers know that they indeed could be like any of the characters in the parable:[24]

- The man traveling from Jerusalem to Jericho is almost completely passive in the parable, but Thurman's retelling gives him some agency during the thieves' attack: "He resisted, apparently, so they injured him."
- Thurman says that the thieves did not intend to beat the man, but attacked the man only because he resisted them, an interpretation that removes the gratuitous nature of their violence.
- The responsibility of the priest is lessened when Thurman states that the priest "did not take any cognizance of his presence or condition."
- Similarly, the Levite "walked by without paying any attention to the destitute man."[25]

Thurman's retelling of the parable, in effect, reduces hearers' negative perceptions of the priest and Levite. These changes correspond with Thurman's informed view of Judaism, including Jesus as a first-century Jew, how unfairly Pharisees and others were mischaracterized, and Thurman's opposition to malevolent anti-Jewish or anti-Semitic perspectives. The effect of these elaborations thus makes it more likely that his hearers could entertain the possibility that they, too, could act like the priest or Levite in similar circumstances.

Although the sermons by Thurman domesticate the parable, on further reflection they include an important overlooked dimension: loving one's neighbors does not just include loving one's perceived enemies; it also includes loving everyone around us, people that we see and may not see because of our lack of attentiveness and mindfulness and an inability to escape a tunnel vision about ourselves, our own situations, lives, problems, or everyday affairs. Portraying the priest and Levite as villains, for example, distances us from them and thus can reduce the story's realism and weaken its impact on modern readers. More importantly, however, modern interpretations that are too negative often descend as drastically as the road from Jerusalem to Jericho into misrepresentations of Judaism and even anti-Semitism.

As argued in the next chapter, the story itself turns a stereotypical "villain," the Samaritan, into a hero to be emulated; if a "wicked" Samaritan can act with compassion (perhaps even "foolishly" so), how much more so should a follower of Jesus?

8

COMPASSION, MERCY, AND HOSPITALITY

The Samaritan Attends to the Traumatized Man (Luke 10:33–34a)

Hanna Cheriyan Varghese, *The Good Samaritan*, Malaysia.
Used with permission of the family. www.hanna-artwork.com.

> So this man is some poor wanderer who's just come here. We must look after him, for every stranger, every beggar, comes from Zeus, and any gift, even something small, is to be cherished.
>
> Homer, *The Odyssey*, book 6

The parable's briskly narrated plot slows significantly to emphasize the actions taken by the next character who comes down the road. In Greek, *Samaritan* is the first word of the sentence, a position that draws special attention to the fact that a despised Samaritan becomes the hero. If contemporary stories establish a pattern, Jesus's hearers probably would have expected an Israelite to be the third person in a priest-Levite-Israelite triad of characters.[1] Instead, Jesus provocatively chooses a Samaritan, a member of a group at enmity with Jews. Relations between Jews and Samaritans in the first century were generally poor (cf. John 4:9: "Jews do not share things in common with Samaritans").[2] If that is the case, the Samaritan in the parable follows Jesus's admonition in Luke 6:27 to "Love your enemies" by showing love, compassion, and mercy.

While *Samaritan* is the first Greek word of the clause, *was moved with compassion* is the last. This delay builds suspense and heightens the impact of the Samaritan's compassion. The pattern set by the priest and Levite is broken: the priest and Levite "came...saw...passed by"; in contrast, the Samaritan "came...saw... was moved by compassion."

The word *compassion* means "touches the entrails"; the Samaritan is moved deeply to assist the man. The Samaritan's resulting actions clarify the reason why the priest and Levite did not assist the traumatized man: they did *not* have compassion.

The Samaritan's compassion reflects the actions of both God (noted in Zechariah's prophecy after John the Baptist's birth, Luke 1:78) and Jesus (for a widow whose only son had died, 7:13). Such compassion models covenant faithfulness for how to treat one's neighbor (i.e., every human being). The Samaritan thus fulfills the compassionate role that the priest and Levite should have fulfilled as the Law and nature of God demand. The father of the returning prodigal son shows the same compassion (15:20), another crucial link between these two parables. In other words, the Samaritan, like the father of the prodigal son, acts exactly as God would act. He seeks to make the man whole, establishing/restoring community in the process. This correspondence, however, should not be understood allegorically. The story instead argues that the compassion of God and Jesus should be the way of life for everyone who follows the teachings of Jesus.

A key Hebrew Bible context for this parable is often overlooked: 2 Chronicles 28:8–15 (cf. 2 Kgs 6:20–23).[3] In that story, the Samaritan army ("the people of Israel"; 28:8) captures two hundred thousand Judean women and children. When the prophet Oded condemns them for what they have done and warns that the wrath of God would come upon them unless they returned what they had plundered, the army releases the captives to the assembly and they:

> took the captives, and with the booty they clothed all that were naked among them; they clothed them, gave them sandals, provided them with food and drink, and anointed them; and carrying all the feeble among them on donkeys, they brought them to their kindred at Jericho. (2 Chr 28:15)

This context is not a direct parallel, and these "Samaritans" were preexilic Israelite inhabitants of Samaria shortly before the Assyrian conquest of the land, but they clothe those who are naked, have the "feeble" ride on animals (with Jericho as the destination), provide the Judeans food and drink, and anoint them. In Jesus's parable, a Samaritan similarly assists someone considered an enemy. In this way, then, the Samaritan is as much a covenantal Israelite as the priest or Levite, a faithful servant of God who provides God's acts of mercy to the wounded man.[4]

The parable then gives a lengthy (for a parable) description of what compassion-in-action looks like. The parable consists of 105 Greek words: twenty to describe the dire situation; twenty-five to portray the priest and Levite's lack of action; and sixty words—more than half—to accentuate the Samaritan's response.[5] The Samaritan is the only character who speaks in the parable, but the emphasis—note the number of verbs in 10:34 alone—is on what he *did*: he went to the man, poured wine and oil on the wounds, bandaged them, put the wounded man on his animal, and took him to an inn where he provided further care. The next day he paid the innkeeper to take care of the man in his absence, promising to settle the account on his return. The detailed description increases the sense of pathos in the parable's hearers, an effective way of persuading them to act similarly.

Several clues in the parable—such as the animal, the Samaritan carrying oil and wine, his recurring use of the inn—indicate that the Samaritan was likely a traveling merchant.[6] Most hearers of Jesus's parable would consider this a despised occupation filled with notoriously dishonest people, which, if true, further reduces the perceived social status of the Samaritan, highlights his compassionate response, and perhaps antagonizes Jesus's hearers further.

With whom would hearers identify at this point of the story? Would they identify with the wounded man or with the despised Samaritan?

A prerequisite for loving one's neighbor is recognizing that they actually are a neighbor, including seeing them as a fellow human being and not as an "other." The priest, Levite, and Samaritan all *see* the wounded man by the side of the road. The Samaritan is the only one to see him as a human being of equal worth, a fellow child of God who should receive compassion-in-action.

INSIGHTS FROM HOWARD THURMAN

> Every man is potentially every other man's neighbor. Neighborliness is nonspatial; it is qualitative. A man must love his neighbor directly, clearly, permitting no barriers in between.
>
> Howard Thurman[7]

The Love-Ethic of Jesus

Thurman uses the Good Samaritan parable as the first example of how the love-ethic—love of God and neighbor—is central to the religion of Jesus in his chapter on love in *Jesus and the Disinherited*. As the above quote shows, the Samaritan responds "*directly*" [emphasis mine] to the man's human need, loving him as a neighbor regardless of human-constructed barriers. Thurman also includes love for one's enemies in this discussion, noting how Jesus overcame his own biases in his encounter with a Syrophoenician woman, for example, and how he applied his love-ethic to his people's oppressors and enemies—the Romans (again, Thurman includes Samaritans as well).

Thurman's arguments in *Jesus and the Disinherited* are crucial here, because Jesus's message to the disinherited is to "love your enemy." The disinherited and their allies should pursue initiatives that facilitate a common sharing of mutual worth, value, and dignity. Disinherited Black people in the United States, for example, must face the "racial enemy" and create opportunities "for freeing such an individual from his 'white necessity.'" All barriers must be removed because, as noted in chapter 1, Thurman insists that "love is possible only between two freed spirits."[8] This "discipline, method, technique" is not just wishful thinking; in Thurman's view, such an approach can be justly criticized as being too optimistic, putting too much of the onus for action on the disinherited, and, in essence, bringing a pillow to a gun fight. Thurman argued, however, that the privileged need a "shock to the system" to reevaluate their position—none will give it up voluntarily—but it must be done in love. He believed that love was the best means to bring about real change.

Thurman defends his position partly by citing the words of his grandmother after a fight Thurman "won" in his childhood—"Nobody ever wins a fight." Thurman suggests another way: "Perhaps the authentic moral stature of a man is determined by his choice of weapons....Of all the weapons, love is the most deadly and devastating, and few there be who dare trust their fate in its hands."[9] With that understood, nonviolence is an essential aspect of reconciliation between human beings of equal worth because nonviolence affirms the existence of other human beings, whereas violence denotes a will to annihilate the other. The purpose of the "psychological tools" of nonviolence "is to open the door of the heart to what another is feeling and experiencing,"[10] which leads to sympathetic understanding.

Compassion: Its Source and Implications for Human Society

All around us, our Father, there are reminders of Thy
  Presence in our midst:
Pangs of conscience,
A spontaneous impulse to do the kind and gracious
  thing,

The sensitiveness to another's needs,
The great burden of anguish which we feel as we look
out upon the world.
Teach us, O living Spirit, the wisdom to lay ourselves
Bare to Thy scrutiny—that we may reflect Thy life
In the dark places of our minds, hearts and desires;
That we may know Thy courage—and the grounds of
Thy hope
For the children of men.

Howard Thurman[11]

Thurman notes the superiority of compassion over pity and the already ample room in the heart for pity. Pity cannot be trusted; it includes, for example, self-pity, the pity that is combined with pride, arrogance, and cunning, and the pity that can be symptomatic of white supremacy.[12] God, however, is at work enlarging the boundaries of our hearts, making room for compassion: "The awareness that where my life begins is where your life begins; the awareness that the sensitiveness to your needs cannot be separated from the sensitiveness to my needs....Although we want those boundaries to be fixed, when we turn to God in the quietness, God is at work enlarging the boundaries of our hearts."[13]

The love-ethic—and therefore compassion—of Jesus is rooted in "perhaps the most daring and revolutionary concept" known to human beings. God is not just the creative mind and spirit at the core of the universe; God is love: "This is the great disclosure: that there is at the heart of life a Heart." The knowledge and experience of this love of God gives human beings a "vast and awe-inspiring tranquility" that supplies them strength to "move confidently out into choppy seas."[14] Thurman also argues that the ultimate source of compassion is God, and our awareness of God provides the inspiration and impetus for following God's example and showing compassion-in-action with our fellow human beings.

Albert Schweitzer notes that "nothing of real value in this world is ever accomplished without enthusiasm and self-sacrifice," and Thurman's interpretation of that declaration reflects his understanding of the parable of the Good Samaritan. The word *enthusiasm* comes from Greek meaning "God inspired or possessed," and Thurman observes that human beings often make sacrifices because of their enthusiasm for things they believe are more significant than what they give up.[15] We can be God inspired, for example, to give of ourselves to other human beings in ways that are similar to the sacrifices made by the Good Samaritan.

The source of compassion and the necessity for extending it to everyone is grounded in Thurman's belief in the unity of life and in God as the source of all, and it is reflected in Jesus's life and message. The foundation of the religion of Jesus, Thurman insists, is that God is one, all life is one, and religion is one. Just as you cannot worship God and mammon, you cannot separate theory from practice, the means from the ends, and the sacred from the secular. God works in human history, and Thurman argues that when we discover within ourselves the intent and purpose of God our Creator, then we can become coworkers with an active, functioning God. If we do so deliberately, with self-conscious intent, we do not merely *act* religious; we *become* religious, worshipping God and serving God in spirit and truth.

Jesus put forward a creative ideal that the source of all life was God, an ideal that affirms the kinship between not just all human beings but also all living things. As a consequence, Christians should have "a reverential and compassionate attitude towards all forms of life."[16] Inherent in this assumption is the method "by which this dream may be realized in the world" by translating it into practical terms of human experience: love. But love is not sentimentalism; it inevitably involves struggle because the ways in which human societies are organized repudiate the ideas of kinship and the ideals of Jesus.

This "God-inspired" process thus devises both personal and group strategies to combat evils in society, such as attempting to awaken the moral consciences of human beings to both individual and social sins. One cannot condemn evils in society that one encourages in oneself. But this moral persuasion must extend to one's oppressors and to other "enemies" as with the Samaritan. Action is urgent because there is "too much agony, too much hunger, too much poverty and misery everywhere, too many flagrant denials of kinship and brotherhood all along the line. I cannot wait for this thing to work out. Something concrete must be done *now*."[17]

Thurman recommends a drastic shock to tear people away from their "alignments in the kingdom of evil, to free them so they may be given a sense of acute insecurity and out of the depths of their insecurity they may be forced to see their brotherhood with the oppressed." Powerful oppressors who feel secure do not relinquish their advantages voluntarily. Only a disruption such as Jesus telling the rich man to sell all he had and to give the money to the poor creates a climate in which the oppressors "are spiritually prepared to embrace the ideal of Jesus." Jesus shows us that God is love, and this key unlocks the meaning of all life:

> What then is the significance of Jesus? He places before the world an impelling dream, growing out of a fundamental interpretation of the meaning of life—human life—all life; a methodology by which that dream might be translated into living power—in a living community; he points out a dynamic available to men by which they may stand in the universe, and also a power by which they may be able to work out a wide series of anticipations of the new community without inner defilement and without self destruction.[18]

An early example of Thurman's understanding of love, compassion, and community, and how they must result in social action is found in "College and Color," an article he wrote in 1924 while a student at Rochester.[19] Thurman challenges his fellow students to develop a "sympathetic understanding" without patronizing or sentimentalization of others of different races: "an attitude which says that a man of another race is essentially myself, and that I feel toward him fundamentally as if he were myself."

Thurman argues that this outlook derives directly from the commands to love God and your neighbor as yourself that are found in the dialogue between Jesus and the lawyer that culminates in the parable of the Good Samaritan. Thurman decries the racism, both covert and overt, to which Black students were subjected every day and argues, "What a hard time Jesus of Nazareth would have if he matriculated at one of our colleges today!" Thurman urges his fellow students to recognize the value, dignity, and sacredness of all other human beings and to feel and act as Jesus commanded: "*Think of the other fellow as essentially yourself and feel towards him fundamentally as if he were yourself.*" As Thurman declared in a 1928 lecture at Spelman College, the true test of following the religion of Jesus is found in the primary face-to-face relationships in one's daily life.[20] Is one following Jesus's command to "go and do likewise"?

Compassion: Relating One-on-One as Children of God

Although Thurman dwells significantly on addressing the traumas of our fellow human beings, he also argues that on the deepest level—and in practical terms—human need cannot be the main focus of our attention, as his October 7, 1951, sermon on the Good Samaritan parable explains.[21] Thurman argues that the parable breaks down barriers that divide us. One of his academic resources, Buttrick's *Parables of Jesus*, notes that the parable eliminates boundaries and illustrates how we should relate to each other as human beings.[22]

Buttrick also writes that the model for a neighbor's assistance was personal, one-to-one. The Samaritan, for example, tended to the wounded man personally, binding his wounds, pouring oil and wine on them, taking him to the inn, staying the night, and only then delegating responsibility to another: "He might have sat on the committee and directed relief from afar. But in giving help he gave himself." Buttrick stresses the need for collective action, for "proper and commendable" governmental involvement to work to solve societal ills but insists that individuals must be the "wellspring of neighborliness": "Love radiates only as life touches life." Buttrick then argues that such compassion-in-action is a deliberate choice and ultimately stems from the love of God: "The spirit of the Samaritan does not come 'by chance.' It is the bestowment of God—It is His best gift to us."[23]

Thurman significantly extends Buttrick's insights beginning with the point that human beings draw lines to separate and protect themselves from "the impersonal operations" of both nature and society. Societies, for example, make "radical distinctions" between those who "belong" and those who "do not belong," which includes attempting to build positions of security, power, and domination.[24] In this sense, the goals of society and the goals of the religion of Jesus are mutually exclusive. Jesus insists that we are related to other people directly, not to any groups, creeds, or race to which they or we belong. We are related *to them*, one-on-one, as human beings. Addressing human need should not be the focus because it may not be altruistic; it may be a response to our own desire to feel good about ourselves or our expectations to be recognized or rewarded, either in this world or the next, or even as a way to feel superior to other human beings while maintaining our own secure position. Instead, we should relate to one another as human beings, distinct from need or any other positive or negative aspects they have: "Jesus says that's the way God deals with human life. And that's the way we are supposed to deal with human life."[25]

Jesus, Thurman says, shows us that from our own inner core, our "deepest part," we must address ourselves to the inner core of other human beings, their "deepest part," despite both our limitations, where there lies within them "that deep, quivering, pulsing sense of infinite worth and value." Therefore, how we feel about ourselves necessarily relates to how we feel about other human beings: "When I feel this way and I meet you and I relate to you out of my own sense of infinite worth, then I will never settle for any particular thing that I see you do, any particular form by which your life may be manifesting itself" but will instead focus on the truest, most worthful, deepest thing in you, that which "calls into vitality...the same stirring of the same deep quality which is God."

Thurman muses on how society would be affected if we applied this "judgment" in our daily lives, relating to people one-on-one, regardless of who they are and what they have done, and how such an approach would impact society at large. He concludes that "the boundless limitless resources of life and of God" become available to people, giving them wisdom, strength, and techniques so they can learn both individually and collectively "how to make a social order in which the spirit of the living God can breathe, and pulse. This is the destiny of man, as Jesus saw."[26]

As Luther Smith observes, for Thurman true community only exists when transformed individuals act in transformed relationships with one another and upon social structures. The impetus comes from the mystical consciousness of the divine within oneself and the realization that the divine dwells in each human being;

that requires a fellowship of mutual caring and serving and is the basis for social transformation.[27] As readers engage with the surprising elements of the Good Samaritan parable, they are provided an opportunity—if not challenged—to transform themselves or be transformed in deep and significant ways.

Again, knowledge is not enough; it must lead to action. As Thurman notes in a January 22, 1956, sermon titled "Justice and Mercy," when we relate to other human beings in this way, we can begin to participate in a way of living and experiencing a dimension of reality that lifts us into a category of being an "authentic child" of God. We work on these understandings and connections for the rest of our lives, but Thurman states again why he believes the structure of the moral order and reality itself are shaped this way: God is the ground of all the structure, "the integrity of the moral order." And when we establish such relationships with one another, when we are merciful to one another, "the strength of God becomes available to [us] in terms of insight, in terms of endurance, in terms of a benediction of [God's] grace. Justice. Mercy. Mercy. Justice."[28]

These one-to-one, core-to-core relationships establish a human fellowship, albeit an imperfect and sometimes turbulent community, as human beings diligently strive to relate to each other in the ways that Jesus demanded, ways that open a new world of possibilities. Thurman's 1951 Good Samaritan sermon thus ends with questions, suggestions, and a challenge that are typical for his sermons:

> Are you willing to try that? Are you willing to try it really? To work at it? And if you work at it—*really* work at it, despite all the things that we know about the psychology of relations and all the learned things—if you really work at it, you can depend upon this: That there will open up to you, more and more, the strength to keep on working at it. Not to achieve it—that is beside the point—but that is the *assignment of man*, and the degree to which he stays in school and works at it, to that degree it is a reasonable thing to dream about a time when this world will be a decent place for friendly men underneath a friendly sky. Let's try it and see.[29]

9

COMPASSION, MERCY, AND EXTENDED HOSPITALITY

THE SAMARITAN BRINGS THE TRAUMATIZED MAN TO THE INN (LUKE 10:34B–37)

Rembrandt, *The Good Samaritan*, 1633, New York, Metropolitan Museum of Art. Gift of Felix M. Warburg and his family, 1941.

It will be possible then for love as an ideal to become the will of society....Certain attitudes which are now considered exceptional, freakish, revolutionary, and rare, belonging only in certain ministers' sermons or in the Sermon on the Mount, would be day to day life in the world of affairs.

Howard Thurman[1]

The Samaritan took the wounded man to an inn and cared for him there. Such commercial inns were known for being frequented by thieves and prostitutes, and, as Longenecker notes, innkeepers were "distrusted as morally dubious figures."[2] Here, the Samaritan trusts an innkeeper—known for dishonesty—with two denarii to assist the wounded man further, indicating a willingness to pay more.[3] Although some postulate that the Samaritan knew the innkeeper because he may have stayed there frequently, others will add this action to their estimation of the Samaritan's foolishness. The Samaritan went beyond just being kind.[4] At great personal risk, he goes to the aid of a stranger, giving him immediate help and taking complete responsibility for the man's recovery, including a "blank check" to an innkeeper. The Samaritan's mercy was not limited to one compassionate act; he committed himself to ongoing, perhaps lengthy, care of this man in need. As Walter Wink aptly put it, "The Samaritan is prodigal in his care."[5] Love and mercy—compassion-in-action—are enduring commitments of community.

Readers are not told what the innkeeper does, another of this parable's ambiguities. Some readers could expect the innkeeper to pocket the money, neglect the wounded man, and perhaps try to extort additional funds from the Samaritan when he returns. Other readers, however, based on the merciful Samaritan's portrayal (which goes against his negative stereotype) may expect the innkeeper to act against his stereotype of dishonesty and to continue the care of the wounded man.

The extension of this care from the road to the inn reflects the ancient concept of hospitality. The term *hospitality* stems from the Greek *xenia* or *philoxenia*, both coming from the word *xenos*, which means stranger or foreigner.[6] The virtue of hospitality includes welcoming, hosting, and assisting strangers or travelers, which in both Greek and Jewish traditions was connected to the divine (e.g., Heb 13:2; *The Odyssey*, book 6). Abraham, for example, was a paradigm of hospitality, hosting three divine guests in Genesis 18:1–16. Abraham's hospitality reflects the hospitality of God and the way God expects human beings to treat one another. Although hospitality occurs typically in one's home, scholars have extended it to include other relationships[7] such as the love of God and the love of neighbor that the lawyer cites and Jesus affirms as the requirements of Jewish law for inheriting "eternal life" (Luke 10:25–28).

A closer examination of the context in Leviticus 19 of what constitutes loving your neighbor is necessary to understand better how the parable of this compassionate Samaritan affirms and reinforces Jewish law. The passage in Leviticus states that God requires holiness of the people: "You shall be holy, for I the LORD your God am holy" (Lev 19:2). Such holiness involves social responsibilities, since God commands God's people to love all human beings in comprehensive ways (cf. Exod 20:1–17; Lev 19:1–18), including dealing ethically with one's neighbor (e.g., Lev 19:13, 15–17) and the stranger (e.g., Lev 19:10, 33–34). The verse in Leviticus that the lawyer cited that helped precipitate this parable is from Leviticus 19:18: "You shall love your neighbor as yourself." Just a few verses later, however, God commands that resident aliens ("strangers") be treated the same as Israelites:

> The alien who resides with you shall be to you as the citizen among you; you shall love the alien as yourself, for you were aliens in the land of Egypt. (Lev 19:34; cf. Deut 16:12)

Leviticus 19:34 repeats God's command in Leviticus 19:17–18 with a critical change in wording (noted in italics below):

> You shall love *your neighbor* as yourself. (19:18)
> You shall love *the alien* as yourself. (19:34)

The acknowledgement that Israel had been strangers in Egypt is fundamental to Israel's identity, and thus a concern for the stranger/resident alien (as well as widows and orphans) is central to the Torah in general, to the Book of Deuteronomy in particular, and should be central, as Deanna Thompson argues, to the community of faith today: "In other words, the strangers are treated like integral members of the community. This ongoing and dogged concern with the welfare of the stranger is a hallmark of Israel's history. And God's people reflect God's concerns."[8]

This hospitality, Jesus argues, should extend to all human beings, even to those deemed as "outsider," "other," or "enemy." The parable portrays a despised Samaritan demonstrating what it means to love one's neighbor. Again, the detailed description of the Samaritan's compassionate actions for the wounded man reinforces what Jesus had said earlier in Luke, to "love your enemies, do good to those who hate you" (6:27). In effect, this parable eliminates the lines separating friend and enemy: "being a neighbor knows no boundaries."[9]

Like the father in the parable of the Prodigal Son, the Samaritan acts as God would act (e.g., Exod 34:6–7) and as God demands God's people to act in Jewish tradition, showing mercy and giving assistance to those in need, even to one's enemies (e.g., Exod 23:4–5). As Zimmermann notes, such actions in the Hebrew Bible reflect God's "steadfast love, justice, and righteousness in the earth," for "in these things I delight, says the LORD" (Jer 9:24; cf. Isa 1:17; Jer 7:5–7). Other texts include complementary attributes and actions such as kindness and mercy (e.g., Zech 7:9),[10] with perhaps the clearest expression of human responsibility in one verse:

> [God] has told you, O mortal, what is good;
> and what does the LORD require of you
> but to do justice, and to love kindness,
> and to walk humbly with your God? (Mic 6:8)

INSIGHTS FROM HOWARD THURMAN

For many years it has been (the desert dweller's) custom to leave a lighted lantern by the roadside at night to cheer the weary traveler. Beside the lantern there is a note which gives detailed directions as to where his cottage may be found so that if there is distress or need, the stranger may find help....To him it is not important who the stranger may be, it is not important how many people pass in the night and go on their way. The important thing is that the lantern burns every night and every night the note is there, "just in case."

Howard Thurman[11]

Hospitality

After Thurman writes about the desert dweller and his lantern, he relates a story about walking along a road near (what is now called) Yangon, Myanmar. At intervals along the way, Thurman found water and fruit provided by Buddhist monks to comfort and bless any passing stranger. Thurman then observes, "The fact that I was a traveler from another part of the world, speaking a strange language, and practicing a different faith, made no difference [to them]. What mattered was the fact that I was walking along the road." Thurman's meditation then closes with a gentle challenge to, in our own ways and along our own paths, leave lanterns with notes along the way, to leave cool water and a bit of fruit, to assist strangers in need.[12] In other words, to live our lives as Good Samaritans and as parents of prodigal children.

Thurman's interpretations of the parable of the Good Samaritan do not dwell on the innkeeper; however, it seems clear that Thurman would not see the Samaritan's trusting of the innkeeper as foolish, but rather as an attempt to extend and build community, similar to how Longenecker envisions the Samaritan's extravagant (and perhaps foolish) "mutuality of trust" and cooperation with the innkeeper. This mutuality involves the fact that the Samaritan has to trust the innkeeper's integrity that he will care for the wounded man, and the innkeeper has to trust the Samaritan's integrity that he will compensate the innkeeper for any expenses over two denarii.[13] In addition, the burden of responsibility for caring for the traumatized man—which may still be significant—shifts from the Samaritan's compassion-in-action to, one hopes, the innkeeper, or, to put it another way, "it becomes a burden that others in the community must share."[14] In this way, community is extended through enlisting, encouraging, and empowering others to act with the same compassion.

As Thurman envisions the process, care for others may begin with an individual but it then extends into communal support. The innkeeper becomes another example of someone to emulate in light of Jesus's call to "go and do likewise," extending the process of being a neighbor into communal support and action. As Longenecker concludes about the Samaritan and the innkeeper, "It is from this risky, fragile and exceptional association that goodness flows to the benefit of the disadvantaged," something that is even more illustrative of how human relations should work in the reign of God, including the command to love one's enemies. If two such questionable and dubious characters can form a productive relationship, how much more should those who claim to follow the teachings of Jesus and the law of God?[15]

The Ultimate Source of Empathy Is God

In a meditation, "Thine Is the Power!," Thurman argues that the ability and strength to assist others comes from God, and one source is "the power that comes from the challenge of a great need, deeply felt, in the lives of others."[16] Although he insists that human need cannot be the main focus of our attention (see chapter 8), in the face of great need, we can forget our limitations, inadequacies, and even our own needs. When we are exposed directly to the needs of others it can "take us out of ourselves, out of our complacency, and put our resources and ourselves completely at their disposal." In some respects, the challenge of the need itself brings the energy and the power to help others, and in doing so "we become something more than we were before."[17] Our own resources are limited, but God continues to be our succor and strength.

Thurman adds more insights about empathy and its source in God in his "Mysticism and the Experience of Love." The greatest aspect of the "imagination" working to understand the contexts of other human beings is its function as the *angelos*, the messenger of God, where one authentically works to put oneself in the place of another human being, and then, as a result, shares the necessary resources to meet those needs. This struggle to identify with another is often glibly conveyed by such sayings as "walking in another's shoes," but instead, this experience should include being "rocked to one's foundations" in ways that force us out of our customary preoccupation with ourselves. Although we can never fully know others' situations, Thurman argues that empathy is an inherent part of creating community: "To be to another human being what is needed at the time that the need is most urgent and most acutely felt, this is to participate in the precise act of redemption." In the process, when our imagination acts as God's *angelos*, we, like the Good Samaritan, may indeed become God's *instruments*.[18] In a meditation about human love, Thurman stresses that

> imagination is the creative vehicle that carries one spirit into the dwelling place of another. There could be no sympathy in the world if men had not the gift of imagination...[and] the witness of God's spirit in men's spirit is symbolized by imagination, without which there could be no sense of sin, no repentance and contrition, no tenderness and sympathy, no love and no hope.[19]

The endeavor to understand people in their contexts and to get behind their actions to the real center of their persons means that we can respond in ways that are more complete and redemptive. In the process, we establish "psychological distance" between them and their deeds—and between their deeds and us—and we come to a mutual understanding of the impact of those deeds on them, ourselves, and others. In doing so, we have to look beyond their faults and even their virtues and persevere, no matter what, in loving them unconditionally. Thurman concludes,

> It is for this reason that there can be no love apart from suffering....It is our faith that this is the way God deals with us....There is no thing outside ourselves, no circumstance, no condition, no vicissitude, that can ultimately separate us from the love of God and from the love of each other.[20]

This process should not be sentimentalized, because people we try to understand and help will remain good and bad, including those who are, for example, greedy, mean, vicious, deceitful, or ungrateful. Yet to act as God does, the followers of Jesus of

Nazareth must love everyone, including their enemies, for God makes the "sun rise on the evil and on the good, and sends rain on the righteous and the unrighteous" (Matt 5:43–48). One's natural inclination is to return hate with hate, but Jesus insists that his followers move to loving even one's enemy, to being a Good Samaritan.[21] Although not sentimental, Thurman was optimistic, an optimism born of his conviction that because the way the universe was constructed, the contradictions in life, even when evil seems to be winning, are not final.

CREATING COMMUNITY ONE-ON-ONE

> Labour well the Minute Particulars, attend to the Little ones....
> He who would do good to another, must do it in Minute Particulars
> General Good is the plea of scoundrel, hypocrite & flatterer.
>
> William Blake, *Jerusalem*[22]

Almost two decades after publishing *Jesus and the Disinherited*, Thurman preached a sermon at Hennepin Avenue United Methodist Church in Minneapolis, Minnesota, titled "Jesus and the Disinherited: The Strength of Love." In that sermon he disabused the audience that it was possible to "love humanity." There is no such thing as *humanity*, Thurman argued, because "humanity has a name, lives on a street, eats, breathes, loves, dies, gets sick, gets hungry; this is humanity." Thurman illustrated this fact with an anecdote about his ten-year-old daughter who told him to stop treating her like a daughter, because, as she said, "A daughter doesn't exist. I'm not a daughter, I'm Ann...and I want you to treat me as Ann, so that in my relationship with you I will feel that I'm here—I'm here."[23]

Following Jesus's command to "go and do likewise," then, means being a neighbor in every sense of the word, accepting and working with human beings who are of equal worth and dignity as fellow children of God. As a negative example, Thurman related the hostility generated inside him when as a youth he had to accept clothes sent in so-called missionary barrels. Thurman therefore stresses that it is a *person* who is in need, and a key issue is how to meet the person's needs without undermining the integrity of the person:

> It is a matter of the profoundest kind of spiritual sensitivity to be able to help, to rescue, a human being in a manner that will enable that human being to forgive you for being able to help him....It is a spiritual quality to feed a hungry person so that the hungry person knows that *he* is being addressed, not merely his hunger....The way my life is conditioned and projected I have to feel that the person who is helping me knows that I am there. Not just my hunger is there; or my nakedness is there. But *I* am there.[24]

Thurman makes clear that we cannot love in general; we must love in particular: to truly love one another, we must know the "facts" about each other, facts that "provide contents for the feeling toll of love that moves from me to you." As David Garland notes, the Greek idiom in the lawyer's response to Jesus ("The one who showed him mercy"; Luke 10:37) is most often understood as doing mercy *to* or *for* another, whereas a better way of translating Luke 10:37 is "he did mercy with him." Acting in this way means having compassion with—suffering with—and having mercy *with* people, which "always makes us vulnerable."[25] Most of Thurman's sermons on the Good Samaritan parable focus on our connections *with* and responsibilities *with* other human beings, as we exist and work with others in community. The transformation of society ultimately depends on the transformation of individual human beings. This personal transformation—experiencing and actualizing the presence of God in one's life—includes building human relations and true community through the life, message, and personal example of Jesus of Nazareth.

For Thurman, building community begins with individual relationships and then extends beyond to create "family." In a 1956 sermon on the Good Samaritan parable in a "Religion of Jesus" series, Thurman shares insights about our relatedness, our community, and our family that are based on the God-centered religion of Jesus. Thurman notes that Jesus proclaimed that one's true family was determined by working relationships (e.g., Mark 3:35: "Whoever does the will of God is my brother and sister and mother"). Essential to this community is Thurman's insistence that we act as Good Samaritans because we are truly children of God in a sacred community of humanity. We are not related by race, creed, or nationality, and we should not act simply because there is need, no matter how great: we act because we become involved in an encounter from the core of ourselves to the core of other human beings—from one child of God to another child of God—an inward community that then manifests itself as an outward community.[26]

Furthermore, Jesus expects God to invade "the normal processes of life," and God's "revolutionary" purpose beginning with the creation of human beings is to establish God's "kingdom of persons, united in the intent to be to each other not only what God would have them to be, but what God is to each other." If this does not happen, Thurman declares, "even though I may say my prayers, bow my knees before the altar, profess the regeneration of the heart in the redemption of my life, I am not a follower of the religion of Jesus."[27]

Becoming "Apostles of Sensitiveness" and "Eccentric Apostles"

In Thurman's concept of community, he envisioned "apostles of sensitiveness" leading the way. In his book *Deep Is the Hunger*, Thurman describes the qualities of apostles of sensitiveness by citing part of the thanksgiving in Paul's Letter to the Philippians: "And it is my prayer that your love may be more and more rich in knowledge and all manner of insight, enabling you to have a sense of what is vital" (Phil 1:9–10a, Thurman quoting James Moffatt Bible). So, apostles of sensitiveness must know what is vital, what is best, and have "a basic and underlying awareness of life and its potentialities at every level of experience."[28] Such apostles are highly empathetic of other human beings; inclusive of all human beings, rejecting prejudices and barriers; recognizing the fundamental unity of all life; and knowing that the contradictions in life are not final.[29]

Barbara Brown Taylor updates this phrase to "eccentric apostles" because "'sensitive' can mean 'delicate' in our time, and apostles are not that." Their receptiveness (or sympathetic understanding) can make them seem eccentric, making them nearer to the growing edge than to the center, even though they often are at the center of things. Thurman is a sterling example of an eccentric apostle in his leadership style and in the ways he led worship services. In these roles, he continually attempted to break down any barriers that separated one form of life from another.[30]

A critical part of being an apostle of sensitiveness/eccentric apostle is, as Thurman loved to say,

> meeting people where they are, *and treating them from there* as if they were where they ought to be. By doing so, one places a crown over their heads that for the rest of their lives they are trying to grow tall enough to wear. To have a highly developed sense of fact with regard to other people is the searching demand of our faith, if we are to be in the spot which we occupy—Apostles of Sensitiveness.[31]

Establishing Community through Practice

Thurman's quest for the Good Samaritan parable's obliteration of human-erected boundaries began very early in his career. During his seminary years, he worked in the summers at a church in Roanoke, Virginia. The summer of 1924, one Sunday afternoon at a young people's meeting at the church, a Muslim from Africa said in regard to segregated churches that "in the Muslim religion there would be no such distinction made.... Allah laughs aloud in his Muslim heaven when He beholds the Christian spectacle: First Baptist Church colored! First Baptist Church White!"[32] As discussed in chapter 2, Thurman sought to eliminate such "in-groups" and "out-groups" in the Fellowship Church in San Francisco by transforming individual human beings, building a community that arose from that transformation, and working toward transforming the larger society.

Thurman's own vision of social transformation was an interfaith vision that extended beyond Christianity. Even though worship services at Fellowship Church and, later, Marsh Chapel, remained largely Christian, Thurman's goal was to move toward a common faith—not *religion* but *faith*—as his 1953 sermon on the mystics of the Upanishads and Bhagavad Gita states:

> At least from my point of view it is hardly a reasonable hope that there should ever come a time in human history when there shall be one world politically and socially until men find out how they can be sustained by one faith. And by one faith I do not mean one creed, one doctrine, one dogma, one church, but one faith, one pulse beat that is so fontal, so—that is so basic to all of the movements of life that it is capable of feeding all the little heartbeats and recognized as such.[33]

Affirmation Mysticism and Social Change

In his 1939 lecture "Mysticism and Social Change," Thurman details how an individual's mystical experience should lead to changes in interpersonal relationships and to social change. He cites Rufus Jones's term *affirmation mystic* to describe people whose mystical experience compels them to "work out" that mysticism with social realities and activism in response to human need. Thurman argues that affirmation mystics join socialists and people "seeking the fullness of the vision of God" who agree with a quote from Eugene Debs: "While there is a lower class, I am in it. While there is a criminal element, I am of it. While there is a man in jail, I am not free." In other words, distinctions between personal selfishness and social selfishness—and personal and social religion—"must forever remain artificial and unrealistic."[34]

According to Jones, mystics are driven to achieve the good they experience in their moments of mystical visions. They should also realize that social problems can never be solved merely by the transformation of individuals, but people who are transformed are responsible for meeting the human need around them in their efforts to achieve the good, alleviating the needs of victims who are suffering because of circumstances beyond their control. The greatest form of service for others is *disinterested service*: "a kind of service that has no narrow ulterior motive at work," one in which the person being served is not some means to an end.[35] The goal of social action is to lessen or remove those circumstances—such as misery due to greed and exploitation—that prevent other human spirits from sensing the good and the divine. Changing those circumstances does not guarantee that they will, but it heightens that possibility because by addressing those social ills, those persons are recognized as people of worth and dignity, and they attain (greater) *agency* over their circumstances.[36]

The steps that Thurman recommends in this 1939 lecture will sound familiar. First, mystics must align their own spirits, even the most stubborn, recalcitrant aspects of them, with the God they experience in their mystical unions. Second, because of their own faults, they must be charitable to the weaknesses of others and compassionate toward them. Third, as members of society, mystics working for social change share consciously or unconsciously the collective guilt of their age and must work out "atonement for this guilt" in ways that are redemptive. Moral appeals to others are the most obvious, but such appeals are only effective on those who share similar visions of the meaning of human life. Preaching to others is apt to be a waste of time and effort, and applying some shock to the system, particularly to oppressors, is often necessary: "Some method must be achieved by which the sufferers in the situation can act so as to shock the oppressors into a state of upheaval and insecurity." Only then will oppressors recognize the oppressed as persons and begin to work toward true equality and community. Affirmation mystics, however, refuse to resort to violence to achieve this shock to the system because they recognize that seeds of destruction are inherent in the nature of evil, and the ultimate end of life is being "worked out through long weary stages in the revelation of God in the progress of history."[37]

Love, Empathy, Community, and Society

An essential element of Thurman's interpretations of the love commands in Judaism—the ones emphasized by Jesus and illustrated in the Good Samaritan parable—is that deeds of loving kindness must occur both individually and communally. These love commands do not merely involve individual acts of mercy and lovingkindness; they involve the transformation of institutions of society. In fact, Thurman calls the understanding that Jesus speaks merely of individual acts "one of the most potent fallacies of the Orthodox religion." In his 1937 lecture "The Significance of Jesus II: The Temptations of Jesus," Thurman speaks of the half-truth that the world can only be made good by individuals becoming good. When the framework of societal relationships remains evil in design, even "saved souls" doing "good deeds" remain functionaries in that evil system.[38] Individual acts of compassion must extend into social acts of compassion and of justice, including acting against structural injustice.

Thurman outlines this envisioned progression from love to empathy to community and then society in his 1938 "The Perils in Preaching the Love Ethic of Jesus."[39] He begins by defining *love* as "the intelligent, kindly, but stern expression of kinship of one individual for another, having as its purpose the maintenance and furtherance of life at its highest level." Self-love, Thurman adds, serves the same function for the individual: the maintenance and furtherance of one's own life at the highest level. Since all life, Thurman argues, arises out of one common ground—God—all expressions of life in their various forms are inherently drawn to one another, and every movement toward increasing cooperation among them is an act of God. Violence, on the other hand, becomes "atheistic," because it denies the unity of life and destabilizes life's maintenance and furtherance at that highest level. That is why hatred and bitterness, which can on the surface appear to be self-validating and create some form of chimeral community, tend to destroy not just the "hated" but also the hater. At this point, Thurman argues, we recognize more clearly Jesus's words about love being the "normal ethical relationship" between human beings that reflects the mind and heart of God. This love must therefore extend from oneself and include all of God's creation.[40]

In this early work, shortly after his transformative experiences in India, Thurman extrapolates a more radical vision of what such love means for society as a whole. For example, since one cannot serve God and Mammon (and one should not worry about what to eat, drink, or wear; Luke 12:6–7, 22–31; 16:13), people should work toward a society in which private property becomes increasingly unnecessary, because only in a society that guarantees the security of every individual can love become the norm and not the exception:

> It seems to me, therefore, that the Christian in the modern world is called upon to dedicate his efforts towards the managing of social life on this basis. This does not guarantee that love will follow automatically, but it will provide a psychological climate and a social framework in which love can fulfill itself.[41]

We should strive to create a society, then, where the actions of the merciful Samaritan, like the father of the prodigal son, should no longer be considered "exceptional, freakish, revolutionary, and rare";[42] they should be the norm, since they are found in the very heart and mind of God.

CONCLUSION: THE GOOD SAMARITAN AS PARABLE; WITH WHOM DO WE IDENTIFY?

> If we love God with all our being, every human being becomes our neighbor, and we are to be neighbors to all.
>
> Dmitri Royster[43]

The lawyer asks Jesus, "Who is my neighbor?" (Luke 10:29), and Jesus responds by telling a story that illustrates what a neighbor is like. The answer to the lawyer's question is the person who was robbed and left for dead. Anyone in need is our neighbor. But in 10:36, Jesus asks a slightly different question: "Who proved to be a neighbor?" The answer to that question is the Samaritan, an answer the lawyer was reluctant to give, saying only, "The one who showed him mercy."

The words "showed him mercy" emphasize *compassion*, the same compassion that God shows (e.g., Luke 1:78) and that people who emulate God show (e.g., 7:13; 15:20) in concrete acts of mercy for human beings, for neighbors, and for "enemies." In the Gospel of Luke, almost every act of mercy comes from an act of God or God's agent, Jesus (e.g., 1:47–50, 54, 58, 72, 78; 17:13 18:38–39; cf. 16:24).[44] The ability to have and show empathy for another human being demonstrates God's love. Or, as Thurman would add, we relate to another human being from our inner core to their inner core, acknowledging the presence of the divine in both.

"Go and do likewise." Jesus's final response to the lawyer encourages readers to identify with the despised Samaritan. Who *proved to be* a neighbor? Act like that person.

What about the priest and the Levite? Whatever view readers initially might have of priests and Levites, after the parable relates their lack of compassion, readers do not want to identify with them. Yet is their selfish or uncaring behavior so unusual? Their seemingly callous inhumanity is indeed something very human,[45] including the rationalization that their inaction was prudent under the circumstances along that dangerous road. We aren't supposed to identify with the priest or Levite, but how many times have we acted like them? Their failures are our own, which explains in part why Christians over the centuries have read this story in anti-Jewish or anti-Semitic ways—ignoring their own complicity, misplacing the blame on Jews or Judaism, becoming self-righteous, not admitting that the parable holds a mirror up to all its readers. As Sylvia Keesmaat states, those who claim to be followers of Jesus are "firmly on the list of those who should be most challenged and threatened by Jesus's parables," including Jesus's concerns about "the most marginalized in our society," and his view of the kingdom embracing even our "enemies."[46]

Thurman's humanizing elaborations of the priest and Levite thus hit their mark. Perhaps Thurman's insights were sparked by Buttrick's comments about the priest and Levite: "Can we be sure that we would never play their part? Perhaps they were 'too busy' with other good works. Perhaps they shrank, as we naturally do, from 'getting mixed up' in such a case....There were a hundred good excuses for their callousness."[47]

Buttrick also writes about the human connection, saying that all too often we label other human beings in ways that make them outsiders, wrapping ourselves in excuses justifying our ignorance and selfishness and "rarely does our sight pierce beyond the accidents of wealth or poverty. Rarely do we discover a *human*....The stricken man was brother to the Samaritan because the stricken man also was human."[48] As Zimmermann puts it, the combination of the love commands just prior to this parable shows that the "relationship to God and the relationship to humans belong together and should not be separated from one another." The ability to empathize—"suffer with" another human being—becomes the decisive element in understanding relationships with other humans, the law, and ethics itself.[49]

In Luke 10:25 the lawyer asked, "What must I *do* to inherit eternal life?" After the parable where the Samaritan shows mercy to the traumatized man, Jesus gives the final answer, "Go and *do* likewise" (10:37). The Samaritan provides the example to emulate, because he emulated the love, compassion, and mercy of God, like Jesus did. The love of neighbor—including one's enemies (Luke 6:27–28, 35)—flows directly from God's love for us and our resulting love of God and for ourselves as children of God.

Charles Hedrick writes that when he identifies with characters in the parable, he is "always" the wounded man—whether receiving pettiness or kindness from others—occasionally is the priest or Levite, and "never" in reality has been the "frighteningly idealistic" Samaritan whose "outlandish, unexpected, and radical behavior challenges [his] own acts of charity."[50] Here Hedrick's candid response connects with Thurman's musings about the limitless human need in the world and how burnout or "compassion fatigue" can easily occur to those who do not match the excessive grace the Samaritan exhibits. Hedrick notes that emulating the Samaritan's response would both exhaust him and his resources, even if he could face taking the risks the Samaritan took. In addition, the parable assaults our prejudices as viciously and perhaps more unexpectedly than the robbers who assaulted the wounded man, including our assumptions that we are right, and others are wrong.[51] Being a merciful Samaritan is easier said than done, if not impossible, but, Jesus says, "what is impossible for mortals is possible for God" (18:27).[52] Thurman would agree, reaffirming that the strength of God becomes available to us.

In the parable of the Good Samaritan, sometimes we may feel we are attacked and in need of compassion and mercy. Sometimes we pass by a traumatized person, without compassion-in-action, pretending we don't notice. But the parable challenges us to be the Samaritan, to risk more than we usually dare, to have both compassion and mercy, to stop and help, and to give more than can usually be expected of us. *We need to make it a habit to go and do likewise, to have attitudes and behaviors that currently only belong "in certain ministers' sermons or in the Sermon on the Mount" but that should be the pattern of life in the world Jesus envisions.*

The truth of a parable is not the moral we stick on the end. It is a story that we live out every day of our lives. The parables that Jesus tells are not just about traumatized people, priests, Levites, and Samaritans; they are about us. We should see more than a message; we should see ourselves, and we should see God.

Jesus told the lawyer to go and do likewise; we do not know how the lawyer responded. We can only know how we respond.

Part V

From Prodigals to Compassionate Samaritans

10

"WE'RE CONNECTED"

Painting of penguins by Howard Thurman, Howard Thurman Meditation Room, Sale Hall, Morehouse College, Atlanta, Georgia. Used with permission of Anton H. Wong and Suzanne Mari Chiarenza.

"Islands"

O for God's sake
they are connected
underneath

They look at each other
across the glittering sea
some keep a low profile

Some are cliffs
The bathers think
islands are separated like them

Muriel Rukeyser[1]

The younger son was a toddler, just learning to talk. One day he uttered some words that were incomprehensible to his parents, but his older brother, not quite five years old, quickly "translated" his brother's words. When the parents realized that the older brother had indeed understood what his brother was saying, they asked him, "How did you know what he said?" The older brother replied, "Because we're connected."[2]

Howard Thurman began painting in San Francisco at the urging of the artist Peggy Strong, whose portrait of Thurman still hangs in the Thurman Lounge of Boston University's Marsh Chapel. Thurman writes in his autobiography that his "greatest joy" came from painting penguins.[3] Sue Bailey Thurman commented that this pastime took Thurman away from his problems, and the Howard Thurman Collection at Boston University's Howard Gotlieb Archival Research Center includes artifacts from this fascination with penguins, including a quote from Paul Richard, annotated by Thurman with a single word: "Truly":

Emperor penguin adults go without eating for nearly three long dark winter months. Such a sacrifice is needed to hatch eggs in frigid Antarctica.

Life requires a constant working together in helping those we really care for: This holiday season, enjoy remembering what we have done together and for each other.[4]

CREATING COMMUNITY

Thurman's greatest legacy may be his vision of an inclusive community. His vision of community is based on reconciliation which recognizes and celebrates the underlying unity of life and the inter-dependence of all life forms. Justice and a sense of innate equality are ruling principles for this community. And the love-ethic establishes and maintains the community's creative character. Personal identity is affirmed while unity is sought with one's fellows.

Luther Smith[5]

As Thurman said in the November 19, 1950, sermon in "The Religion of Jesus and Social Change" series, the religion of Jesus is God-centered and has both inward (vertical) and outward (horizontal) dimensions. When we turn our "inward eye" to God, God becomes the answer to all our needs. This vertical dimension provides each individual believer a basis for whole, integrated action, since all one does takes on meaning and significance from God, "the center out of which they come"—including the horizontal dimension of one's relationships with others. One reason for Jesus's command to love one's enemies and to do good to them is "in order that you may become children of your Father" (Matt 5:44–45). That is the way God treats human beings and how God wants human beings to treat each other; the command to love is "the key to the whole structure of the religion of Jesus." This perspective has critical implications for social change, because Christians are called, like God, to see beyond the good and evil in people and to relate to their center, to their "very spirit." We can forgive any evil they have done to us, because we go beyond their actions—whether good or bad—and relate to them as fellow human beings.[6]

In his November 26, 1950, sermon in the same series, Thurman declares that this "horizontal" dimension of our relations with other human beings is a "sense of participation in a collective destiny," that we are not alone in our commitments, struggles, triumphs, and failures; we are part of a community; we have a profound sense of belonging. And within the fellowship that we have with others, such as in the Christian church, there is an insistence that the boundaries of the fellowship should expand—not in the spiritual and ethnic arrogance of the missionary movement within historical Christianity, but instead the idea that "I cannot be satisfied in Heaven if my brother is in Hell....I cannot be at peace in my wholeness, if you are in part; I can never be what I ought to be until you are what you ought to be. For better or for worse, we are involved in a single creative encounter." When we widen the sense of our participation in a collective destiny, we include all human beings, not just those who "bow their knees at my kind of altar." As we include more people, all of whom are of infinite worth as children of God, we discover no *profound* difference between us. Each of us must find the place that our abilities and attributes will allow us to engage most effectively in the transformation of society, in "giving my life as an outgoing expression of the religion which I have experienced in the community." We may or may not be successful as individuals, but we should dedicate ourselves to be a person on whom "God can depend."[7]

Thurman's experiences—even in the midst of the difficulties he faced—led him to believe that there was a spirit abroad in life—and Christianity is but one expression of it—that ultimately leads to wholeness and community.[8] Religious experience not only opens the door to God, it opens the possibility of hearing the sound of the genuine in other human beings: "One man's response to the sound of the genuine in another man is to ascribe to the other the same sense of infinite worth that one holds for oneself. When this happens, men are free to relate to each other as human beings."[9] In other words, we are free to live and act as the father of the prodigal son and the merciful Samaritan—to love God with all our heart, soul, strength, and mind, and to love our neighbor as ourselves.

WHY BE GOOD? BECAUSE IT IS GOOD

One of the more optimistic of Thurman's ethical perspectives is that human beings should do good simply because it is good, not for any sense of reward or fear of punishment. Thurman's meditation "Shall I Be Good?" begins, for example, with a quotation from a Naylor sonnet: "Shall I be good because of some reward, because the virtuous act pays dividends?"[10] Thurman explores how to escape from the tyranny of reward and punishment, expecting "to be rewarded because we are good and punished because we are bad." He argues that morality should not be located outside of us, and that even though people sometimes reap what they sow, such is not always the case. Doing what is virtuous sometimes does not pay dividends:

> In the last analysis, men cannot be persuaded to be good because of the reward either here or beyond this "vale of tears." Men must finally come to the place in

> their maturity which makes them do the good thing because it *is good*. Not because it is a command, even a divine command, but because the good deed, the good thought, the good life is in *itself good*.

Reward and punishment should thus be irrelevant, and Thurman states "I shall be good because it is *good*."[11]

And yet there is more here: Striving against the forces of evil not only puts one "on the side of the good thing because it is good" but also anticipates the kingdom of God, which assumes, or hopes, that the many and sometimes overwhelming contradictions in life that one encounters are not final, that there is a spirit in human beings and the world always working against the things that hurt and destroy. There is always the hope that living wisely and courageously on the side of good will allow others "who see the sunlight in [your] face...drop their tools and follow" in your footsteps,[12] which leads to another critical assumption in Thurman's thought: we are all one.

WHY BE GOOD? BECAUSE WE ARE ALL ONE

Thurman often spoke of the difficulties of building and maintaining community and the fact that disputes and conflicts are inevitable. To understand another human being requires dedication, hard work, time, effort, and diligence.[13]

Because God is the ground of our being, Thurman argues that human beings have two areas of need. The first is something to worship. The second is to be part of the human family. Human beings are not separate units of existence; rather, they are involved in a collective experience of human aliveness that drives them to develop and maintain lines of communication with other members of the human family. The best communication is done with warmth, love, and fellowship. Human beings can resort to hate and belligerence, but these shouts of anger ironically reveal the underlying desire of one's heart for kinship and community. Thurman thus stresses how human beings must realize that there is but one human family created by God and that all are members.[14] Like the brothers in the story at the beginning of this chapter, *we are connected.*

Thurman expands on the nature of human connectedness in his meditation, "We Are All One." He begins by quoting Plotinus: "If we are in unity with the Spirit, we are in unity with each other, and so we are all one" and then he affirms the underlying unity of all life, with the "Spirit of God" being both the unifying principle and the most crucial experience of human beings. This experience leads to a fundamental aspect of ethics, such as noted in 1 John 4:20–21, that if people say they love God whom they have not seen and do not love the other who is with them, they are liars. People who love God must also love their brothers and sisters. Unfortunately, Thurman observes, many people who appear devout in their worship of God belong to some of the "most terrifying hate organizations," but, as Plotinus reminds us, the test of whether we are in unity with the Spirit of God is whether we are in unity with one another. We can never be at peace with God if we are not at peace with other human beings: "For the sake of my unity with God, I keep working on my relations with my fellows. This is ever the insistence of all ethical religions."[15]

We seem to be "our most true selves" when we are deeply involved with others, relating to them in common understanding and part of a common faith, building community outward to include other human beings. Since human community has been ruptured, forgiveness and restoration play a crucial role; they bridge relationships between groups through personal relationships among individuals of those differing groups. Personal relationships are crucial, because the souls of human beings feed on them, and they are the door through which we enter "into the Holy of Holies where God dwells. For behold the dwelling place of God is in the hearts of men!"[16]

Thurman also addresses the difficulty of maintaining a gracious spirit when contending with injustice. A gracious spirit, he makes clear, is not cowardly or sentimental, because we must oppose the brutal and terrifying presence of evil in the world. Yet every judgment is a self-judgment; we are not innocent, so we should seek to promote a gracious spirit within ourselves as we contend with injustices.[17]

The means by which Thurman envisioned the creation and maintenance of community with diverse human beings is similar to one found in a 1952 study by R. D. Minard that illustrates how animosity and conflicts between white and Black miners were not evident when they were working underground in the mine.[18] Deep in the mine, they identified as "miners" first and foremost. Convincing people that they belong to "a single superordinate group" can help eliminate hostility and create community. The question remains: Is creating, sustaining, and extending such a community possible?

WHY BE GOOD? FOR OUR OWN GOOD

As Thurman's *Jesus and the Disinherited* argues, the hounds of hell—fear, deception, and hate—often triumph over Jesus's message of love—his teachings about justice, reconciliation, restoration of community, and the resulting humanitarian actions toward all people. Adam Serwer's seminal essay "The Cruelty Is the Point" illustrates that some political discourse in the United States thrives on viciousness against people deemed "outsiders," disinherited people who serve as convenient scapegoats to blame for the ills in society or, at least, perceived slights, grievances, or "persecution" against the "in-group." This rhetoric and cruelty help bind the "in-group" into a "community" fueled by fear, deception, and hatred that celebrates punitive actions against marginalized people who, in their eyes, "deserve it." The blame is misplaced, but it is difficult to persuade people who hold such grievances otherwise; the truth is unsettling to them.[19]

Thurman made similar observations over the course of his career, and the ill effects of hatred was an essential concern in his *Jesus and the Disinherited*. Another example is found in *The Luminous Darkness*, where he writes about how unsympathetic understanding can easily become ill will and hatred. On one hand, hatred "may become a foundation upon which the personality stands in an effort to establish a dreadful emotional security. It is possible for personal significance to emerge on the other side of hate that becomes a form of self-validation." So hatred becomes an "internal rallying center" for one's personality—giving energy and strength like a form of neurosis—which supports and helps one implement a "position" from which to attack perceived enemies and which even wills their "nonexistence" as human beings.[20] Yet, on the other hand, if human beings accept the idea that all life is one, hate becomes a form of annihilation not only of others but also of oneself. The love-ethic of Jesus, in contrast, is "the intelligent, kindly but stern expression of kinship of one individual for another, having as its purpose the maintenance and furtherance of one's life at its highest level."[21]

When discussing the Black experience in the United States, Thurman often mentions his grandmother hearing the enslaved preacher who assured his enslaved congregation that they were not slaves but were precious in the sight of God, the same as every other human being (see chapter 5). That, Thurman argues, is the contribution the religion of Jesus makes to humankind.[22] We are assured that God, the Creator of the world, loves and cares for us, and that all other human beings are our brothers and sisters, a fact that should supply us with enough "energy to support a universal morality, a universal brotherhood."[23] Jesus speaks so much about love because by necessity the disinherited must begin by practicing love in their small group of oppressed people. Loving other Christians, having socially redemptive encounters with each other, is the first step because "Christian morality" means feeling an obligation to include others, embracing those "outside," just as the original Pentecost did. Christians thus should be "a leaven at all levels of the community and in public and private living."[24] This describes what Thurman tried to accomplish during his long and distinguished career.

In some respects, then, Thurman appeals to self-interest, because, as Luther Smith notes, Thurman believed that the "self can only find fulfillment in a loving community, and a loving community is only possible when individual selves are given the opportunity for their fullest possible nurture and expression."[25]

THURMAN'S VISION: THE PRODIGAL SON BECOMES A COMPASSIONATE SAMARITAN

The foundation of Thurman's philosophy of community is one's relationship with God. Thurman's mysticism led him to understand that one's experience with the divine not only drives one to act in love but that acting in love maintains that relationship with the divine. In his 1978 lecture "Mysticism and Social Action," Thurman speaks of how important this is for the disinherited. He stresses that he is "an outsider in the community of power," because as a Black man in the United States he faced oppression and persecution, and he found it necessary, as he put it, "to find within myself the door that no man could shut, to locate resources that are uniquely mine, to which I must be true if the personal enterprise of my life is to be sustained." In this way, every person in times of distress "can affirm one's significance and place."[26] Mysticism, Thurman notes in this lecture, insists that every person has inside them the ability to defend themselves against this "grand invasion." They can seek within themselves to grow in the experience of solitude but alongside the minds and spirits of other mystics. Thurman cites, once again, his experience as a young boy, communing with nature—the sand, the sea, and the stars.

His encounters with nature were primary experiences of God within one's "personal inner core."[27] A total response to this encounter transforms the inner quality of one's life as well as its outward manifestation. Thurman stresses once again that this impetus comes from the divine within us: "The insistence is not so much that something invades the life of man from without but rather that through the quietness and inner solitariness the individual becomes conscious of what it is that he has in him all the time. Be still and *know* that I am God."[28]

It is here that Thurman's interpretation of the core message of the Prodigal Son parable—that when the prodigal "came to himself," he came to the father—leads inexorably to the core message of the Good Samaritan parable—to "go and do likewise" as the Samaritan had done.

In addition to the other arguments he musters for standing alongside and aiding our fellow human beings in need, Thurman points to another, internal reason: social action is also resistance against whatever tends to separate us from the experience of God.

> Therefore, the mystic's concern with the imperative of social action is not merely to improve the condition of society....The basic consideration has to do with the

removal of all that prevents God from *coming to himself in the life of the individual.* Whatever there is that blocks this, calls for action.[29]

Thurman insists that "whatever there is that blocks the way to my own altar" or to the other person's altar must be removed. Thurman is alluding to Matthew 5:22–24, where Jesus says that even being angry with a brother or sister makes one liable to judgment, so before offering a gift at the altar, you must first reconcile with your brother or sister.

Why does Thurman include "the other person's altar" in his arguments? Whenever injustice or oppression occurs, both the sufferer and the offender are cut off from their own altars, and Thurman insists, "I am under obligation to identify with each." We do not just identify with the hungry, poor, and others who suffer, but also with "those whose power, privilege, and insensitivity are largely responsible for the social ills" that stand between them and their altars.

Here is where loving one's enemy can be misunderstood, because "one of the radical functions of social action" is to make offenders aware of the consequences of their offenses. Love is not a warm, fuzzy feeling about one's neighbor or enemy; love is taking concrete actions for their betterment. Thurman argues for "some form of shock." Moral persuasion is usually not enough to make people aware of what is at stake. Therefore, offenders must be jolted into "an acute sense of the same kind of insecurity" that their actions are causing for other people in society. Thurman cites as an example a boycott against an unscrupulous grocer by Operation Breadbasket in Chicago. The people affected first tried to convince the grocer not to sell spoiled, inedible food, but when no amount of talking worked, they started a boycott. One of the participants said about the grocer, "We do not wish him any harm particularly, but he must be forced to *feel* what it is like to be victimized and defenseless." This "shock treatment" holds up a mirror to oppressors that reflects to them images of those who suffer at their hands and allows them to have a sympathetic understanding of others, with a central concern of removing any obstacle preventing them access to the altar in their hearts.

In other words, people should not just act like the compassionate Samaritan; they should also work to make sure that the priest and the Levite are able to identify and sympathize with the traumatized man and "go and do likewise."

Thurman correctly focuses on the love and compassion of the father of the prodigal son and the good Samaritan, but it is also critical to explore the ambiguous aspects of the two sons and the innkeeper. In the Prodigal Son parable, *both* sons must respond in ways that reestablish community with their father and with each other; the responsibility lies on their shoulders to respond to the love and compassion of their father. In the parable of the Good Samaritan, the innkeeper *must* respond and build community by extending the compassion and mercy of the Samaritan. The open-ended characterizations of the two sons and the innkeeper stand as challenges to the readers and hearers of the parables to act in ways that repair and build community with concrete actions, just as much as the compassion-in-action of the father and the Samaritan does.

"FRIGHTENINGLY IDEALISTIC" AND UNREALISTIC?

> It can be argued that Thurman's vision is noble, but it has an unrealistic means. The struggle for justice may be a more appropriate concept for achieving community than the ethic of love.
>
> Luther Smith[30]

Critiques of Thurman's optimistic view that the contradictions of life are not final can be compared to Charles Hedrick's response to the Good Samaritan as being "frighteningly idealistic." Does the arc of history ultimately bend toward justice[31] because God is good and the creator of all things?

The ongoing quest for justice must play a foremost role in the quest for civil and human rights and for true community; hence the admonition "no justice, no peace." Thurman's emphasis on Jesus's love-ethic, influenced in part by interaction with Reinhold Niebuhr and his thought (e.g., *Moral Man and Immoral Society*), includes the idea that both individuals and social structures had to be transformed. In a commencement address at

Morehouse and Spelman Colleges in 1932 at which Thurman gave the benediction, Niebuhr cautioned that "power makes selfishness," and "a disinherited group" like African Americans would never win full justice in society by "patient negotiation from a position of inferiority."[32]

Niebuhr's perspective is crucial, because, as Luther Smith notes, Thurman's optimism—where "good is more compelling than evil"—"is one of Thurman's most vulnerable tenets."[33] Such critiques, then, are both important and necessary,[34] but it should also be noted, as do Smith and others, that Thurman knew very well the tragedies of human striving against oppression. He had no illusions, for example, "about the size and scope of the obstacles that stood in the way of black equality."[35]

Thurman himself sometimes struggled to maintain his optimistic perspective. For example, in March 1970, Thurman and Sue Bailey Thurman traveled by sea through the South Pacific and Asia during a low point in Thurman's life. Thurman recorded some reflections that mirror our contemporary society's problems, derived from the same issues of racism, prejudice, patriarchy, and oppression:

> Where are we headed? We are deeply troubled...we are internalizing the hostility and the hate by which we have been surrounded for so many years. Something in the soul has gone sour....
>
> We are losing our compassion. After all, what does compassion mean? The quality to feel with another and this is different from feeling *for* another. If I can manage to feel with another this makes me available to him whatever of wisdom and resources that are uniquely my own. I place myself at his disposal and this means I trust him not to undertake my destruction. If in his desperation this is what he does then I must protect him and myself from catastrophe.[36]

Thurman then muses over what makes violence so bewitching; it gives human beings an illusory sense of omnipotence because for a moment they have the power of life or death over another. This illusion briefly satisfies the ancient hunger to control and master one's environment.

At least two aspects of this belief should be examined. First, if we assume a sense of omnipotence is temporary, we can see specific instances of power and control of others as impermanent, but often when one power falls another one takes its place. Second, that leads to the question, Can the ancient hunger to dominate others be alleviated when one learns or believes that it is indeed illusory and brief? History, so far, appears to reflect that it does not; human beings either have not learned that such power is temporary or, if they have, it does not matter to them. As a result, Thurman's despondency over the situation in 1970 is understandable.

We can see Thurman's realism interspersed with optimism in many places, including in a sermon near the end of his life. On October 26, 1980, he preached what was likely his last sermon at probably his last public appearance. He spoke from his former pulpit at Fellowship Church a sermon titled "The Growing Edge," a title he had used many times before. In this sermon, Thurman focuses on the question at the heart of community that was central to his vision not only of Fellowship Church but of the religion of Jesus: "whether it is possible to develop a caring, sensitive, loving community in a world organized on violence and brutality and hate."[37] Some of Thurman's despair is evident in the sermon:

> The burden of proof is on our weary shoulders. The day is long and the night is very hard but if we can't do it maybe God [break in the audio]. And my only prayer is that He will not get tired and give us up. If so, where shall we go? So, while we have a chance. Let's try again and again and again.[38]

These words from Thurman speak directly to our current situation more than forty years later, but they are not the final word. We know from his decades of writings, lectures, and sermons that Thurman, no matter how weary he became, clung to the hope that, despite appearances, such contradictions in life were not final.

11

GOING FORWARD

"We All Do Better When We All Do Better"[1]

The Good Samaritan with the Merciful Armies of Love, © 2022 Janet McKenzie. www.janetmckenzie.com. Collection of Carlow University, Pittsburgh, PA.

> Compassion is the source of true joy, peace, and happiness. It is the foundation of a good heart, the essence of a meaningful life, and the fundamental principle for creating a better world.
>
> The Dalai Lama[2]

This chapter honors Thurman's contributions and suggests some ways to move forward in light of the insights gleaned from his body of work, including the interpretations of the parables of the Prodigal Son and the Good Samaritan. This chapter can also serve as an afterword for those who remain unconvinced of Thurman's mystical perspective of the unity of life and the role of a creator, or those who reject the concept of God or the supernatural altogether, or who are skeptical about Thurman's nonsectarian perspective on religion that envisions Jesus not as a savior but as an example among others who "walked with God," or those who are looking for a light at the end of a very long tunnel of disappointment. Or, perhaps, it will address those who, like Thurman in his final sermon, believe in a divine presence but are despondent over the ways in which evil often succeeds in our world, wondering whether their task to make the world a better place is a Sisyphean endeavor.

We are living during another era of "white rage," where advances toward equality and equity for African Americans—as well as other Black, Indigenous, and people of color—have been met with concerted, relentless efforts to roll back that progress.[3] Yet Luther Smith correctly reminds us that although each generation has new and distinctive challenges to face, it is not just a disservice but an insult to previous generations, especially those who suffered under horrific oppression—with enslavement, Jim Crow laws, lynchings, and countless other acts of cruelty—to believe that our situation is worse than theirs and that Thurman's message is therefore irrelevant. Smith also notes that we can argue about some details about his "common ground" conclusions—and Thurman would welcome that debate—but

> what is required of us now is to live into that prophetic vision of common ground and to embrace its radical consequences. To repeat Thurman's conviction that each of us has the responsibility and the ability to fulfill our prophetic calling: we have no valid excuses to withdraw from committing ourselves to the realization of common ground. None![4]

One key question is this: Can enough people be persuaded to love their neighbors as themselves to make a real difference in society? Or an even more foundational question: Can I convince myself to love my neighbors as myself?

Perhaps an appeal to virtue is the place to start—that being a virtuous person is an end in itself. Thurman noted, for example, that a decision to strive for virtue can be taken from a philosophical perspective, not just a religious one.[5] To do good because it is good. Yet how many people have trodden that path successfully?

An appeal to love your neighbor *as yourself* can include one's self-interest. Thurman argued, for example, that although hatred and the other hounds of hell—fear and deception—can give people a false sense of significance, purpose, and community, the hounds of hell ultimately destroy the hater from within. In this world, however, the question *Why do the wicked prosper?* remains relevant, because the hounds of hell often appear successful.

Thurman believed that the ethics of Jesus cannot be separated from his religion and also that a "parochial religious experience" (e.g., Christian-only) cannot sustain a universal ethic. His philosophy, and as Luther Smith states, some of Thurman's comments, suggest that religious experience with the divine—like the one experienced by Jesus but not exclusive to him—may be the "only hope for community."[6] Yet the utility of loving one's neighbor as oneself also can be defended whether or not religion—perhaps *faith* is a better word—is taken into account.

A RELIGIOUS OR SECULAR UNIVERSAL ETHIC?

Lobsang Tenzin Negi sees extensive parallels between Thurman's apostles of sensitiveness/eccentric apostles and Buddhist teachings in the search for common ground.[7] One key connection is the Dalai Lama's vision for a secular, universal ethics with which both "religious and nonreligious people" can work toward creating "a friendly world underneath friendly skies."[8] The Dalai Lama's vision for extending compassion for all includes two pillars: (a) being aware of our common humanity and (b) realizing our interdependence. The key is to move away from a focus on self toward a desire to see others flourish (love) and to alleviate the suffering of others (compassion). Negi concludes,

> [The Dalai Lama] does not see spirituality as a strictly religious practice, but rather a practice of basic human values such as love, compassion, forgiveness, and tol-

erance that are shared by both the religious and non-religious....Secular ethics is complementary to all the major faith traditions in that it emphasizes concern for others' well-being.[9]

Thurman's perspective on Buddhism was complex; he saw some aspects as congruent with his philosophy and theological perspective—and saw similarities between the Buddha and Jesus—but other aspects he found incompatible.[10]

Also incompatible but containing some correspondences with Thurman's thought is a "secular" evolutionary approach to universal ethics. Frans de Waal, for example, argues that we can have morality without religion, that morality is older than religion, that it exists for evolutionary purposes, and it is therefore ingrained in the human psyche. Religions came later and incorporated, adapted, and codified the morality already in existence. A key aspect of de Waal's arguments is that morality exists among animals for the same evolutionary reasons, and he proposes that it consists of two tenets: (1) reciprocity combined with a sense of justice and fairness, and (2) compassion and empathy, even in the face of, or sometimes because of, an often-brutal world that includes power, aggression, and domination. Human morality also is an "evolved morality," de Waal states; although more developed, it exists in continuity with other primates (e.g., empathy and consolation, prosocial tendencies, and reciprocity and fairness).[11]

Such research fascinated Thurman, and he sometimes cited scientific studies to bolster his own arguments for religious experience and the unity of life. Another relevant aspect of de Waal's work is the incorporation of decades of research that shows that animals can learn to cooperate, a cooperation that involves reciprocity and empathy.[12] Numerous studies, of course, show that human beings, religious and nonreligious, also can develop empathy and compassion in ways that change people, relationships, organizations, and cultures. One key aspect of research specific to the topic of this book is that *storytelling*—another positive aspect of parables—can increase understanding of and empathy for another.[13] Researchers have also discovered that not only can empathy be developed but that such growth can be sustained over long periods of time. This long-term growth in empathy requires *chronic, repeated experiences and practice.* Such a result brings to mind Thurman's thoughts about community requiring unifying experiences that were multiplied over extended periods of time.[14] One of the groundbreaking researchers of these studies, Tania Singer, used insights from Buddhist monks—who believe that empathy and compassion can be developed—to investigate whether the ancient techniques used by those monks could "tune people's brains for kindness." She and over seventy other researchers conducted a two-year study that sought to develop empathy through training people in meditation, focusing on others, and practicing empathy. The researchers discovered striking differences in behaviors and practices and, in addition, "found that empathy-related parts of the brain grew in size after kindness training....Singer's team showed for the first time that through purposeful effort, people can build long-term empathy and, in the process, change their biology."[15] Research has also suggested, that among "non-human vertebrates," spite is "virtually absent."[16] Human beings may be the only animal—and definitely the primary one—to act with spite, and, as Thurman argues, acting in spite, prejudice, or hatred is detrimental to everyone.

One way Thurman illustrates how injurious spite and hatred are to community is by citing Olive Schreiner's "The Sunlight Lay across My Bed." In that story, a person dreams that God took her to hell, which seemed a beautiful place, with singing birds and blue water. In this apparently peaceful setting, the woman notes,

> We stood looking and I saw [men] working among the bushes, digging holes, but in the holes they set nothing. And when they had covered them with sticks and earth, each man went a way off and sat behind the bushes watching. And I noticed that as each walked, he set his foot down carefully, looking where he stepped. And I said to God, "Why do they do that?" And God said, "They are making pitfalls into which their fellows may sink." And I said to God, "Why do they do that?" And God said, "Because each man thinks that when his brother falls, he will rise." And I said to God, "How will he rise?" And God said, "He will not rise." And I saw

their eyes gleam from behind the bushes. And I said to God, "Are these men sane?" And God said, "They are not sane. There is no sane man in hell."[17]

A WEB OF MUTUALITY

Heather McGhee in her book *The Sum of Us* also shows how fear, deception, and hate—elements of racism, for example—demonstrably harm almost everyone, not just their intended targets. Racist white people in the United States, for instance, tend to operate from a zero-sum perspective of "us" against "them," believing that whatever is good for "them" is bad for "us." Yet, McGhee notes—as did Thurman and writers from James Baldwin to Toni Morrison—"racism is a poison first consumed by its concocters." This zero-sum game perspective only benefits a small group of wealthy individuals. What most people do not realize is that the oppression of the "other," of the disinherited in society, usually is a "canary in a coal mine." In other words, the systems exploiting those with their backs against the wall usually expand to exploit other groups as well. Those people who support oppression because it only hurts the "other"—and falsely believe it helps them—ultimately find themselves similarly oppressed by the powerful.[18]

McGhee documents a paradigmatic case: the desegregation of the 1950s resulted in many local communities closing their public swimming pools because they did not want their Black neighbors to use them, which meant that white families lost that public resource as well. Montgomery, Alabama, for example, not only closed the public pool—they filled it with concrete—but also shuttered every public park, sold the animals in the zoo, and padlocked the community center.[19] Those whites with adequate funds joined private pools or built swimming pools in their yards, but the public pool closings across the United States made what was once a public resource into a "luxury amenity."[20]

McGhee provides many examples where policies instituted or reinforced by white racism not only hurt the targets of such racism but also work against "non-wealthy white Americans"—most white people in the United States—whether it involves social welfare programs, health care and health insurance, higher education,[21] or other public programs that benefit everyone. In the states that refused to expand Medicaid, for example, a higher *percentage* of people of color struggle more, but the *number* of white people harmed is higher.[22]

A SOLIDARITY DIVIDEND

McGhee observes, similar to Thurman, that exploitative practices against other human beings are made possible by an "in-group" severing the human tie between them and other human beings (the disinherited "out-group" deemed the "other"). This exploitation is rationalized by the social distance that results from the "in-group" being unable or unwilling to empathize with the group they are exploiting.[23] And, as Thurman notes, wealthy people (the privileged) are not usually disturbed and moved to action when the "other" (e.g., the disinherited) suffer. Such privileged people assume that their wealth, which protects them from one kind of suffering, will also protect them from other kinds of suffering.[24]

Instead, McGhee argues, a healthy, functioning society rests on the foundation of a "web of mutuality," a sense of social solidarity, "a willingness among all involved to share enough with one another to accomplish what no one person can do alone." The result is a "solidarity dividend" of benefits for all in society when people of all races unify and work together for their common good.[25]

McGhee describes one example of such a breakthrough moment that occurred to Bridget (a white woman who worked at a Wendy's in Kansas City) during a meeting of fast-food workers who were organizing in support of a higher minimum wage: "When a Latinx woman described her life...Bridget was moved. 'I was really able to see myself in her. And at that point, I decided that the only way we was gonna fix it was if all of us came together. Whether we were white, brown, Black, it didn't matter.'"[26] Bridget no longer was operating from an "us against them" zero-sum game.

Perhaps such arguments will convince some people to "come to their senses" like Thurman's depiction of the prodigal son, but we will still be far from creating a beloved community.

In 1949, Thurman preached a sermon, "The Quest for Peace," in which he argues that the quest for peace involved working for a social situation envisioned in Micah 4:4, every person could "sit under [their] own fig tree and be unafraid."[27] The preceding verses in Micah 4 include the famous quote, "they shall beat their swords into plowshares" (4:3), and Thurman speaks of eliminating violence and establishing peace through the "work of righteousness." As Gandhi had noted, issues of poverty and hunger cripple people's abilities to work nonviolently for social justice. Another key insight of Gandhi, Thurman argues, is that peace is the "byproduct of righteousness, of social and economic justice." We work for "social righteousness" so that every person can sit under their own fig tree and be unafraid, providing a climate of mutual trust, and working "in the tremendous business of trying to get a world in which an ordinary human being can keep his self-respect and be alive...in which little children can grow up without fear."[28]

A VIRTUOUS SPIRAL: THE PRODIGAL SON AND GOOD SAMARITAN PARABLES

The Samaritan's actions in the parable of the Good Samaritan set a daunting standard, as do the father's compassion and forgiveness in the Prodigal Son parable. These two parables, however, say that the father's forgiveness and the Samaritan's compassion-in-action should be the norm for how human beings treat all other human beings, how to love God and love your neighbor as yourself.

THE FATHER AND HIS TWO SONS: FORGIVENESS AND HAPPINESS

The parable of the Prodigal Son leaves ambiguous whether the prodigal repents. In addition, the father welcomes his son back joyfully, without any mention of punishment or even admonishment. The ambiguity of the parable (unlike its context in Luke) suggests that the same extravagant, forgiving, loving actions should be offered whether the son was repentant or whether he was still trying to manipulate his father for his own benefit.

Amy-Jill Levine, for one, finds in the parable a simple exhortation that is "more profound" than a message of repentance and forgiveness: do not wait for an apology or for the ability to forgive someone who wronged you. Instead, "Do whatever it takes to find the lost and then celebrate with others, both so that you can share the joy and so that the others will help prevent the recovered from ever being lost again."[29]

The actions of the father are unusual, but they are the idealistic goal Jesus sets for human relationships, and they set the standard for how the older son—who is also estranged from his father—should act, even though the parable does not supply his ultimate response. Here again contemporary evidence shows that such forgiveness benefits not only the people who are forgiven but also the ones who forgive. One recent study conducted in five different countries finds that when forgiveness is learned and implemented, those practicing forgiveness achieve greater happiness, better mental and physical health, including reductions in anxiety, depression, blood pressure, and other positive outcomes such as better sleep. *The study appropriately notes important exceptions: someone in an abusive relationship, for example, should seek safety elsewhere as soon as possible.* In most cases, however, as Andrew Serazin notes, "the science is clear that it works. It helps the people who are doing the forgiving....[But] that doesn't mean you can't seek justice....It doesn't mean there are no consequences."[30]

The Good Samaritan: Compassion-in-Action and a Virtuous Spiral

The Samaritan in the Good Samaritan parable, like the father in the Prodigal Son, is a paradigm of God's compassion-in-action that Jesus embodies and commands his followers to go and do likewise.

McGhee argues that such altruistic Good Samaritan behavior can create a web of mutuality and a solidarity dividend that benefits all of society, and her conclusions correspond with the results of the "World Happiness Report."[31] The report concludes that the greater the instances of altruism—helping another person without expecting anything in return—the higher level of happiness results in both those helped and those helping. This outcome is still present when compared across various nations and across individuals. Furthermore,

> the causal arrow also runs in the opposite direction. Experimental and other evidence shows that when people's well-being increases, they can become more altruistic. In particular, when people's well-being rises through experiencing altruistic help, they become more likely to help others, creating a virtuous spiral.[32]

Evidence thus strongly suggests that "paying it forward" is effective. McGhee believes that a functioning society depends on a "web of mutuality" of social solidarity; Jesus says that true community is built by working actively for the well-being of all other human beings—loving all our neighbors—which ultimately includes our own well-being. Unfortunately, those words have been little heeded over the intervening centuries, but the evidence strongly suggests that communities and even societies can create a "virtuous spiral" through individuals and groups voluntarily "paying it forward." To do so does not mean the elimination of self-interest, just a greater focus on the interests of others.

COMPASSION-IN-ACTION, JUSTICE, AND EXTENDING COMMUNITY

Thurman sometimes cautioned his congregations not to overstate the correspondences between the world of a parable and the actual world, whether in the first century or our own. In his sermon "Poverty and Riches," for example, when he discusses the parable of the Rich Man and Lazarus, he states, "Don't make the parable walk on six legs; just let it walk on four."[33]

One example of making the parables of the Good Samaritan and Prodigal Son "walk on six legs" is to turn them into allegories;

another way is to assume they show the entire fabric of Jesus's teachings, not just one key thread. The Good Samaritan, for example, depicts a "frighteningly idealistic" and perhaps even foolish compassion-in-action. The Prodigal Son portrays a father foolish enough to give a son his inheritance without any hesitation and then to forgive his wayward returning son without punishment. In light of that forgiveness, it is not foolish to ask, "But what about justice?"

In asking that question, we are perhaps in danger of becoming like the elder brother in the Prodigal Son parable, unless we, as Christopher Marshall argues, work toward "compassionate justice" with the knowledge that true justice, restorative justice, can only be achieved through the conscientious cultivation of compassion.[34]

Marshall sees the parable of the Prodigal Son as a narrative of restorative justice, but such restoration requires contrition, confession, change of life, and atonement or reconciliation. The Good Samaritan parable serves to complement the restoration of the prodigal, because it demonstrates the restoration of an innocent victim, and, for Marshall, the Samaritan not only serves as an exemplar of individual altruism, but "there are also intimations...of the need for structural and systematic transformation."[35] This call to respond, as the next section explores, is echoed in Thurman's interpretations.

CONCLUSION: THE CALL TO RESPOND BECAUSE OR IN SPITE OF IT ALL

> We are not trapped or locked up in these bones. No, no. We are free to change. And love changes us. And if we can love one another, we can break open the sky.
>
> Walter Mosley[36]

The ambiguities of the responses of the two sons in the Prodigal Son and the innkeeper in the Good Samaritan serve an important purpose. Unanswered questions about their responses, just as much as the compassion-in-action of the father and the Samaritan, challenge readers and hearers to act in ways that repair and build community. Readers and hearers of these parables must decide how the sons and the innkeeper should respond in ways that allow true community to emerge and expand, and they should respond similarly in their own lives.

The ambiguity of whether the younger son repents is answered by the context of Luke and the history of responses to the parable. There is also no doubt in the Gospel of Luke and in the history of interpretation as to what response the older son is supposed to have, and the same goes for the innkeeper. The responsibility for restoring community, in response to their father, rests upon the shoulders of both sons, just as responsibility for extending community, in response to the Samaritan, rests on the shoulders of the innkeeper. In this way, both parables extend these responsibilities to the shoulders of all interpreters of the two parables.

The younger son, in Thurman's estimation, would be driven to examine himself and repent. The son had to "purify himself of the self-judgment" that resulted because of his violation of the loving relationship between him and his father. He had to "redeem his life" from his self-inflicted lacerations to "work out his salvation" in his father's household.[37] Thurman in this sense agrees with Christopher Marshall's interpretation of the Prodigal Son parable as compassionate, restorative justice that necessarily involves the (re)creation of community.

As Thurman explains further in *The Creative Encounter*, the impetus for this reorientation is not as dependent on God requiring it than that people feel shame about some attitude or attribute in the presence of God:

> It is not due merely to a demand which God makes of me, but it is rather due to a recognition of the fact that there are those qualities of personality, those attachments to things, those desires that succeed in blurring the vision and limiting the sense which I have of being totally and completely encompassed by the love of God.[38]

So, the prodigal—and all human beings who are similarly estranged—must "repent" in the way that the Greek term for repentance, *metanoia*, designates: a fundamental reorientation and transformation that includes loving God and one's neighbors as oneself. As Thurman puts it, God deals with the prodigal—loves him—at the core of his being, and the prodigal "can now deal with the facts of his own life; and he will seek to introduce all these qualities into his relationships with his fellows."[39] And "his fellows" certainly includes his older brother. The justice demanded by the older brother cannot be achieved through retaliation but only through the contrition, confession, repentance, and restoration of his younger brother. Only then can the family sit at the feast in true community.

Just as the compassionate father in the Prodigal Son parable sets the standard for human behavior, so does the compassionate Samaritan in the Good Samaritan parable. In addition, similar to the purpose served by the ambiguities of the responses of the two sons is the open-endedness of what the innkeeper will do. The parable challenges us to provide a response; the one that is certainly expected is that the innkeeper will follow the Samaritan's example, take care of the wounded man, and thus continue to build and extend community.

Similar to the situation that Thurman acknowledged in his final sermon at Fellowship Church in 1980, our current landscape appears bleak, and the hounds of hell seemingly are (again) winning. Thurman offers the religion of Jesus as an example of how to respond, an approach of love that could overcome fear, deception, and hate. The prescriptions of both the Prodigal Son and Good Samaritan parables are idealistic if not unrealistic, but Jesus says the father's and the Samaritan's compassion-in-action should be the goal if not the norm for how human beings should treat all other human beings.

The parables of Jesus challenge their hearers to change their behavior but go much deeper than that. The radical change in behavior results from a radical change in one's worldview.[40] Jesus's parables call for a renunciation of who we believe we are and a reorientation from who we are to who we will be; in other words, we must grow into the crowns placed above our heads.

If we allow the parables of the Prodigal Son and Good Samaritan to speak to us, they invade our lives, challenge us, and become the foundation of new possibilities in our relationships with others. Perhaps they even persuade us to work toward bending the arc of history toward justice, acting in ways that help create a web of mutuality, and participating in an ever-expanding virtuous spiral of altruism. In other words, loving our neighbors as ourselves. Thurman urges us, even when discouraged, to try it and see. As he said in his final sermon at Fellowship Church, "So, while we have a chance. Let's try again and again and again."

NOTES

Abbreviations:

HTC	Howard Thurman Center
JATD	Howard Thurman. *Jesus and the Disinherited.* Boston: Beacon, 1996 [1949].
PHWT	Walter Earl Fluker, ed. *The Papers of Howard Washington Thurman.* 5 vols. Columbia: University of South Carolina Press, 2009–2019.
WATSA Parables?	David B. Gowler. *What Are They Saying about the Parables?* 2nd ed. Mahwah, NJ: Paulist Press, 2021.
WHAH	Howard Thurman, *With Head and Heart* (New York: Harcourt Brace Jovanovich, 1979.

PREFACE

1. Howard Thurman, *WHAH*, 9.

2. Cf. Howard Thurman, *Footprints of a Dream: The Story of the Church for the Fellowship of All Peoples* (Eugene, OR: Wipf and Stock, 2009).

3. As Thurman wrote in his autobiography about his experience at Rochester Theological Seminary when he "was living for the first time in a totally white world"—which also applies to the situation he faced in the dominant society in the United States—"they were at home in this world, and I felt a stranger." *WHAH*, 46, 48.

4. Howard Thurman, "Mysticism and the Experience of Love," HTC Box 3, Folder 9, 18. A version of this idea is also

found in "In His Image": Howard Thurman, *The Inward Journey* (Richmond, IN: Friends United Press, 1971), 120–21. See the discussion in chapter 9.

5. Howard Thurman, "For Meditation," HTC Box 10, Folder 16, k.

6. Howard Thurman, *JATD*, 79.

7. The inability or unwillingness to understand Jesus's status, perspectives, and teachings is especially pronounced among white Christian evangelicals in the United States. See, for example, Anthea Butler, *White Evangelical Racism: The Politics of Morality in America* (Chapel Hill: Ferris and Ferris Books/UNC Press, 2021); Robert P. Jones, *White Too Long: The Legacy of White Supremacy in American Christianity* (New York: Simon & Schuster, 2020); Robert P. Jones, *The Hidden Roots of White Supremacy: And a Path to a Shared American Future* (New York: Simon & Schuster, 2023); Katherine Stewart, *The Power Worshippers: Inside the Dangerous Rise of Religious Nationalism* (New York: Bloomsbury, 2019).

8. Kipton E. Jensen, *Howard Thurman: Philosophy, Civil Rights, and the Search for Common Ground* (Columbia: University of South Carolina Press, 2019).

9. Howard Thurman, *Sermons on the Parables*, ed. David B. Gowler and Kipton E. Jensen (Maryknoll, NY: Orbis Books, 2018).

10. Howard Thurman, "The Desert Dweller," in Howard Thurman, *Meditations of the Heart* (New York: Harper & Brothers, 1953), 90–91.

11. Howard Thurman, *Essential Writings*, ed. Luther E. Smith Jr. (Maryknoll, NY: Orbis Books, 2010), 9. In *Jesus and the Disinherited*, Thurman condemns the "man-dominated social order" that Olive Schreiner attacked, supports the Equal Rights Amendment, and opposes "the morally degrading aspects of deception and dishonesty" such oppression produces between men and women, 49.

ACKNOWLEDGEMENTS

1. Howard Thurman, March 26, 1965, broadcast of *Face to Face* on NBC. Transcribed from the audio of this broadcast

housed in the Special Collections of Emory University's Pitts Theology Library.

2. Mikhail Bakhtin, *Problems of Dostoevsky's Poetics* (Minneapolis: University of Minnesota Press, 1984), 110.

CHAPTER 1

1. Howard Thurman, *WHAH*, 6.

2. Thurman, *WHAH*, 6.

3. Howard Thurman, *Footprints of a Dream: The Story of the Church for the Fellowship of All Peoples* (Eugene, OR: Wipf and Stock, 2009), 15.

4. The following quotes are from Thurman, *WHAH*, 5–9.

5. Thurman, *WHAH*, 6.

6. Thurman, *Footprints*, 18.

7. Howard Thurman, quoted in Luther E. Smith Jr., *Howard Thurman: The Mystic as Prophet*, 3rd ed. (Richmond, IN: Friends United Press, 2007), 40.

8. Thurman, *Footprints*, 17–18.

9. Thurman, *WHAH*, 20.

10. Howard Thurman, "Mysticism and Social Change" (*PHWT* 2:213).

11. Thurman, *WHAH*, 7–8.

12. Thurman, *WHAH*, 8–9.

13. Paul Harvey, *Howard Thurman & the Disinherited: A Religious Biography* (Grand Rapids, MI: Eerdmans, 2020), 15.

14. Thurman, *WHAH*, 36.

15. Howard Thurman, *The Luminous Darkness* (Richmond, IN: Friends United Press, 1989), x.

16. Thurman, *WHAH*, 41. In a May 6, 1980, interview with Eugene Bianchi of Emory University, Thurman notes that this metaphor stems from Olive Schreiner "The Buddhist Priest's Wife" (see *PHWT* 5:307, 311).

17. Thurman, *WHAH*, 46.

18. Thurman, *WHAH*, 51.

19. Thurman, *WHAH*, 83.

20. Thurman, *WHAH*, 132.

21. Thurman, *WHAH*, 127–28.

22. Thurman, *WHAH*, 142.

23. *Life*, April 6, 1953, 126–32.

24. Thurman, *WHAH*, 166–67.

25. Albert Raboteau, "In Search of Common Ground: Howard Thurman and Religious Community," in *Meaning and Modernity: Religion, Polity, and Self*, ed. Richard Madsen, William M. Sullivan, Ann Swidler, and Stephen M. Tipton (Oakland: University of California Press, 2002), 157–58.

26. Cf. Martin Luther King Jr., "My Pilgrimage to Nonviolence," *Fellowship* 24 (1958): 4–9.

27. Howard Thurman, *JATD*.

28. *PHWT* 2:xix.

29. Peter Eisenstadt, *Against the Hounds of Hell: A Life of Howard Thurman* (Charlottesville: University of Virginia Press, 2021), 122.

30. Thurman, *WHAH*, 113–14.

31. Eisenstadt, *Against the Hounds of Hell*, 122.

32. *PHWT* 1:263–70.

33. Noted by Harvey, *Thurman*, 64.

34. Harvey, *Thurman*, 93, 96; *PHWT* 3:xxxi.

35. Thurman, *JATD*, xix.

36. Thurman, *JATD*, 1–11.

37. Thurman, *JATD*, 12, 17. In this section, Thurman is dependent on Vladimir Simkhovitch, *Toward an Understanding of Jesus* (New York: Macmillan, 1947), 60–61.

38. Thurman, *JATD*, 18.

39. Thurman, *JATD*, 23–25. Luther E. Smith Jr., *Howard Thurman: Essential Writings* (Maryknoll, NY: Orbis Books, 2006), 28.

40. Thurman, *JATD*, 26–47.

41. Thurman, *JATD*, 43.

42. Thurman, *JATD*, 45–47.

43. Thurman, *JATD*, 48–63.

44. Thurman, *JATD*, 53–56.

45. Thurman, *JATD*, 58.

46. Thurman, *JATD*, 60.

47. Thurman, *JATD*, 64–78.

48. Thurman's views on how one could defend oneself and one's group in the face of violent oppression were complex, with some development over time, influenced, for example, by the Holocaust and World War II.

49. Eisenstadt, *Against the Hounds of Hell*, 131, 424.

50. Luther Smith, "Prophetic Vision and Its Radical Consequences," in *The Unfinished Search for Common Ground*, ed. Walter Fluker (Maryknoll, NY: Orbis Books, 2023), 23.

CHAPTER 2

1. Howard Thurman, *WHAH*, 269.

2. Howard Thurman, *The Search for Common Ground* (Richmond, IN: Friends United Press, 1986), xiii, 3, 5.

3. Thurman, *WHAH*, 129.

4. Howard Thurman, "The Cosmic Guarantee in the Judeo-Christian Message" (June 1944), HTC: Box 7, Folder 11.

5. Howard Thurman, *Disciplines of the Spirit* (Richmond, IN: Friends United Press, 1977), 104.

6. Peter Eisenstadt, *Against the Hounds of Hell: A Life of Howard Thurman* (Charlottesville: University of Virginia Press, 2021), 356.

7. Luther E. Smith Jr., *Howard Thurman: Essential Writings* (Maryknoll, NY: Orbis Books, 2006), 88.

8. Luther E. Smith Jr., *Howard Thurman: The Mystic as Prophet* (Richmond, IN: Friends United Press, 1991), 50, citing Howard Thurman, *Deep Is the Hunger* (New York: Harper & Brothers, 1951), 109.

9. Smith, *Mystic as Prophet*, 50–51.

10. Smith, *Mystic as Prophet*, 205.

11. Smith, *Mystic as Prophet*, 52.

12. Thurman, *Deep Is the Hunger*, 109. Cited by Smith, *Mystic as Prophet*, 56.

13. HTC: Box 3, Folder 9. Thurman's mysticism also reflects similar insights as found in nineteenth-century transcendentalists such as Ralph Waldo Emerson and Henry Thoreau. See Paul Harvey, *Howard Thurman & the Disinherited: A Religious Biography* (Grand Rapids, MI: Eerdmans, 2020), 103–4.

14. Harvey, *Thurman*, 104–105; Smith, *Mystic as Prophet*, 77–79.

15. Thurman, "Mysticism and Social Change," *PHWT* 2:215.

16. Summarized from Smith, *Mystic as Prophet*, 79–81.

17. Smith notes the similarities here with the perspective of Ralph Waldo Emerson (*Mystic as Prophet*, 100–101).

18. Unfortunately, it was not published until 2009 in *Benjamin E. May*, ed. Samuel DuBois Cook (Franklin, TN: Providence House, 2009), 197–207.

19. *PHWT* 5:154. Thurman viewed the end of Jim Crow laws, however, as more than "superficial change," as noted by Peter Eisenstadt in a personal communication.

20. *PHWT* 5:155–56.

21. *PHWT* 5:156.

22. Eisenstadt, *Against the Hounds of Hell*, 359.

23. Harvey, *Thurman*, 175.

24. "What Can We Believe In?," *PHWT* 5:241.

25. "Desegregation, Integration, and the Beloved Community," *PHWT* 5:156–57.

26. "What Can We Believe In?," *PHWT* 5:243.

27. "What Can We Believe In?," *PHWT* 5:244.

28. This quote is from Thurman's sermon about William Blake from July 10, 1950, in his "Men Who Have Walked with God" series. Howard Thurman, *The Way of the Mystics*, ed. Peter Eisenstadt and Walter Earl Fluker (Maryknoll, NY: Orbis Books, 2021), 12.

29. See David B. Gowler, *The Parables after Jesus* (Waco, TX: Baylor Academic Press, 2020), 164–68; Christopher Rowland, *Blake and the Bible* (New Haven, CT: Yale University Press, 2011).

30. Thurman, *Way of the Mystics*, 10.

31. Thurman, *Way of the Mystics*, 13, 16.

32. Thurman, *Way of the Mystics*, 17.

33. Smith, *Mystic as Prophet*, 9.

34. Smith, *Essential Writings*, 35.

35. Quoted in Howard Thurman, *Deep River and The Negro Spiritual Speaks of Life and Death* (Richmond, IN: Friends United Press, 1975), 6, 125.

36. *PHWT* 1:126.

37. Thurman, *Deep River*, 6, 126.

38. Thurman, *Deep River* (*The Negro Spiritual*), 125-26.

39. Thurman, *Deep River* (*The Negro Spiritual*), 127.

40. Thurman, *Deep River* (*The Negro Spiritual*), 130, 135.

41. Thurman, *Deep River*, 18.

42. Thurman, *Deep River*, 30, 42–43.

43. Thurman, *Deep River*, 47.

44. Eisenstadt, *Against the Hounds of Hell*, 233.

45. Howard Thurman, *Footprints of a Dream: The Story of the Church for the Fellowship of All Peoples* (Eugene, OR: Wipf and Stock, 2009), 90.

46. Thurman, *Disciplines of the Spirit*, 96–98.

47. Harvey, *Thurman*, 179.

48. Amanda Brown, *The Fellowship Church* (Oxford: Oxford University Press, 2021), 149–50.

49. Walter Fluker, "Creating and Cultivating Democratic Spaces," in *The Unfinished Search for Common Ground*, ed. Walter Fluker (Maryknoll, NY: Orbis Books, 2023), 207.

50. Thurman, *Footprints*, 25.

51. Thurman, *WHAH*, 93–94.

52. Thurman, *WHAH*, 95. He says the same thing about his use of the fine arts at Fellowship Church in *Footprints*, 25, 28.

53. Thurman, *Footprints*, 34–37.

54. Thurman, *Footprints*, 65, 69. For additional details, see pages 87–94.

55. Thurman, *WHAH*, 146–48.

56. Thurman, *WHAH*, 95, 147. For a statement of this belief that includes a scientific rationale as well, see Thurman, *The Creative Encounter*, 86–87.

57. Thurman, *The Way of the Mystics*, 12.

58. For more details see Gowler, *Parables after Jesus*, xi–xii.

59. William Blake, *Blake: Complete Writings* (Oxford: Oxford University Press, 1969), 793. The painting, currently in the Philadelphia Museum of Art, can be viewed here: https://philamuseum.org/collection/object/59861.

CHAPTER 3

1. C. H. Dodd, *The Parables of the Kingdom* (Glasgow: Collins, 1961), 16.

2. Octavia Butler, *The Parable of the Talents* (New York: Seven Stories Press, 1998), 19.

3. Approximately half of Rembrandt's earliest works (i.e., from the 1620s) depict people of advanced years. Noted in Mariet Westermann, *Rembrandt* (London: Phaidon, 2000), 51, 54.

4. For an in-depth analysis of these contexts, see Gowler, *WATSA Parables?*, 69–93.

5. Francis Brown, S. R. Driver, and Charles Briggs, *Hebrew and English Lexicon of the Old Testament* (Oxford: Clarendon Press, 1907), 695. A *mashal* can range from a proverbial saying (e.g., "Is Saul among the prophets?"; 1 Sam 24:13) to a song of derision (e.g., the taunt against the rich in Mic 2:4) to a similitude or allegorizing parable (e.g., the boiling pot in Ezek 24:3–5).

6. See the numerous studies discussed in Gowler, *WATSA Parables?*, 75–88.

7. See George A. Kennedy, *New Testament Interpretation through Rhetorical Criticism* (Chapel Hill: University of North Carolina Press, 1984), 10–11; David B. Gowler, "Heteroglossic Trends in Biblical Studies: Polyphonic Dialogues or Clanging Cymbals?" *Review and Expositor* 97, no. 4 (2000): 455.

8. David B. Gowler "The *Chreia*," in *The Historical Jesus in Context*, Princeton Readings in Religions, vol. 12, ed. John Dominic Crossan, Amy-Jill Levine, and Dale Allison Jr. (Princeton, NJ: Princeton University Press, 2006), 138.

9. Gowler "The *Chreia*," 134–38. For a discussion of Greco-Roman contexts of parables, see Gowler, *WATSA Parables?*, 94–107.

10. Adolf Jülicher, *Die Gleichnisreden Jesu* (Darmstadt: Wissenschaftliche Buchgesellschaft, 1963), I.98.

11. T. W. Manson, *The Teaching of Jesus* (Cambridge: Cambridge University Press, 1951), 57–58.

12. Theon's quotation is from *Progymnasmata* 3.

13. Mary Ann Beavis, "Parable and Fable," *Catholic Biblical Quarterly* 52 (1990): 477.

14. Joshua Stigall, "Progymnasmata and Characterization in Luke's Parables: The Parable of the Rich Fool as a Test Case," *Perspectives in Religious Studies* 39, no. 4 (2012): 349–60.

15. Mikeal C. Parsons and Michael Wade Martin, *Ancient Rhetoric and the New Testament* (Waco, TX: Baylor University Press, 2018), 45–70.

16. See Justin David Strong, *The Fables of Jesus in the Gospel of Luke* (Paderborn, Germany: Brill, 2021).

17. Charles Hedrick, *Parables as Poetic Fictions* (Peabody, MA: Hendrickson, 1994), 19–20.

18. See Strong, *Fables of Jesus*, for a discussion of collections of fables extant in the first century CE (e.g., Babrius, Phaedrus).

19. Karl Meuli, "Herkunft und Wesen der Fabel," *Schweiz Archiv für Volkskunde* 50 (1954): 77. Cited and translated by Strong, *Fables of Jesus*, 43.

20. Barbara Reid, *Parables for Preachers*, vol. 3 (Collegeville, MN: Liturgical Press, 2001), 127–31.

21. Noted by Mikeal C. Parsons, *Luke: Storyteller, Interpreter, Evangelist* (Peabody, MA: Hendrikson, 2007), 22.

22. Dodd, *The Parables of the Kingdom*, 16.

23. The parable and its interpretation are based on the discussion in V. N. Voloshinov, "Discourse in Life and Discourse in Art," in *Freudianism: A Marxist Critique* (New York: Academic, 1976), 93–116. I use "Voloshinov/Bakhtin" to indicate that I agree with those scholars who argue that Mikhail Bakhtin played a primary role in authoring this essay.

24. Dodd, *Parables of the Kingdom*, 146.

CHAPTER 4

1. Gerd Theissen, *The Shadow of the Galilean*, 2nd ed. (Minneapolis: Fortress Press, 2007), 54.

2. Gowler, *WATSA Parables?*, 67–68. For an example of a productive interdisciplinary dialogic approach to the parable of the Rich Fool, see the teacher's guide for chapter 4.

3. See the discussion of Thurman's *JATD* in chapter 1. See also William R. Herzog II, *Parables as Subversive Speech* (Louisville, KY: Westminster/John Knox, 1994), 3. Much of following is dependent on David B. Gowler, "'At His Gate Lay a Poor Man': A Dialogic Reading of Luke 16:19–31," *Perspectives in Religious Studies* 32 (2005): 249–65.

4. S. N. Eisenstadt and L. Roniger, *Patrons, Clients, and Friends* (Cambridge: Cambridge University Press, 1984). For an excellent list of the characteristics of such alliances, see K. C. Hanson and Douglas E. Oakman, *Palestine in the Time of Jesus* (Minneapolis: Fortress Press, 1998), 72; for a discussion and examples from ancient literature, see Zeb A. Crook, ed., *The Ancient Mediterranean World: A Sourcebook* (Grand Rapids, MI: Eerdmans, 2020), 45–59, 273–84.

5. See James C. Scott, *The Moral Economy of the Peasant* (New Haven, CT: Yale University Press, 1976), 1, 5, 11, 27, 51.

See also Richard Saller, *Personal Patronage under the Early Empire* (New York: Cambridge University Press, 1982). Saller distinguishes *patronage*, which is a personal interaction, with *benefaction*, which designates an impersonal interaction where the benefactor does not meet the recipients. See 45–59. Although the author of Luke is above the social level of a nonelite ("peasant"), the "voices" of the nonelites (e.g., the artisan Jesus and his first followers who transmitted this parable) still echo dialogically in the parable. See Gowler, *WATSA Parables?* 41–42, 153. Since the term *peasant* is anachronistic as far as the first century is concerned, I use the awkward but more accurate term *nonelite*.

6. Justin David Strong, *The Fables of Jesus in the Gospel of Luke* (Paderborn, Germany: Brill, 2021), 111. Cf. Howard Thurman, *Deep River and The Negro Spiritual Speaks of Life and Death* (Richmond, IN: Friends United Press, 1975); and David B. Gowler, *The Parables after Jesus* (Waco, TX: Baylor Academic Press, 2020), 213–18.

7. Cited by Strong, *Fables of Jesus*, 259.

8. As Ste. Croix also notes, Quintilian's *Institutio Oratoria* (V.xi.19) states that fables have special appeal to "country boors and the uneducated." G. E. M. de Ste. Croix, *The Class Struggle in the Ancient Greek World* (London: Duckworth, 1981), 444. It must be said, however, that the powerful often coopted the fable for their own ends—to maintain their power.

9. Phaedrus, *The Fables of Phaedrus* (Christopher Smart): http://www.perseus.tufts.edu/hopper/text?doc=urn:cts:latinLit:phi0975.phi001.perseus-eng1:1.15.

10. Bernard Brandon Scott, *Hear Then the Parable: A Commentary on the Parables of Jesus* (Minneapolis: Fortress Press, 1989), 19.

11. Cf. Theissen, *Shadow of the Galilean*, 150, and David B. Gowler, "The Four Horsemen of Evangelical Hypocrisy: How They Whitewashed Donald Trump," *Salon*, May 18, 2018, https://www.salon.com/2018/05/18/the-four-horsemen-of-evangelical-hypocrisy-how-they-whitewashed-donald-trump/.

12. Herzog, *Parables*, 27–28.

13. Gowler, *WATSA Parables?* 111–12. On the other hand, Luke uses characters like the Roman centurion who helps the community (7:1–10) or Zacchaeus (19:1–10) as examples to emulate.

14. Halvor Moxnes, *The Economy of the Kingdom* (Philadelphia: Fortress, 1988), 127–28.

15. Jerome Neyrey, "Ceremonies in Luke-Acts," in *The Social World of Luke-Acts*, ed. Jerome Neyrey (Peabody, MA: Hendrickson, 1991), 385.

16. Peter Eisenstadt, *Against the Hounds of Hell: A Life of Howard Thurman* (Charlottesville: University of Virginia Press, 2021), 237.

CHAPTER 5

1. James Weldon Johnson, "The Prodigal Son," in *God's Trombones* (New York: Penguin, 1990), 21.

2. Self-identification with the prodigal's "repentance" is clearly seen in such influential works of visual art as Albrecht Dürer's *The Prodigal Son amid the Swine* (1496), where it seems likely that Dürer portrayed himself as the "prodigal" kneeling in penitence among the pigs. Sometimes, of course, other people or groups are identified as (one of) the two brothers, as is found in Luke's Gospel (15:1–2).

3. David B. Gowler, *Host, Guest, Enemy, and Friend* (Eugene, OR: Wipf & Stock, 2007 [1991]), 250–54.

4. Mikeal Parsons, *Luke: Storyteller, Interpreter, Evangelist* (Peabody, MA: Hendrickson, 2007), 239–40.

5. The Mishnah (which was compiled ca. 200 CE but includes earlier traditions) possibly illuminates some relevant contexts, such as (a) the elder son receives a double inheritance (cf. Deut 21:17); (b) a father could assign ownership of his property to his sons, but he retains property rights during his life; and (c) if the father assigns ownership to his sons and they sell the property, the new owner cannot assume ownership until after the father's death (Mishnah B. Bat. 8:7). Richard Vinson postulates that the latter may apply to what happens in this parable; that the younger son sells the property he inherited. See *Luke* (Macon, GA: Smyth & Helwys, 2008), 508. The son's demand to his father, however, is beyond the Mishnah's context.

6. Cf. Bailey who argues that by requesting his inheritance the younger son in effect is wanting his father dead: Kenneth E. Bailey, *Finding the Lost* (St. Louis: Concordia, 1992), 109; and

The Cross and the Prodigal (Downers Grove, IL: InterVarsity Press, 2005) in which chapter 2 is entitled "The Death Wish" (40–47). Bailey also uses this argument to conclude that "humankind in their rebellion against God really want him dead!" (exclamation mark his; *Cross and Prodigal*, 42). For an argument against Bailey's conclusions based on experiences with contemporary "village groups all across the Middle East," see Carol Schersten LaHurd, "Re-viewing Luke 15 with Arab Christian Women," in *A Feminist Companion to Luke*, ed. Amy-Jill Levine (Cleveland, OH: Pilgrim Press, 2002), 246–68.

7. It also is, for example, against Roman law: Arland J. Hultgren, *The Parables of Jesus: A Commentary* (Grand Rapids, MI: Eerdmans, 2000), 73, citing Fritz Schulz, *Classical Roman Law* (Oxford: Clarendon, 1951), 203–303.

8. Elizabeth Yates, *Howard Thurman: Portrait of a Practical Dreamer* (New York: John Day, 1964), 73–74. Emphasis mine.

9. Thurman was exposed to the academic study of the Bible as early as 1918, and throughout his adult life rejected literalist interpretations of Scripture, rejected some standard Christian dogma, and interpreted the Bible as teaching metaphorical truths; see Paul Harvey, *Howard Thurman & the Disinherited: A Religious Biography* (Grand Rapids, MI: Eerdmans, 2020), 19. His distinctive interpretations of the Prodigal Son sometimes fall into the latter category.

10. Howard Thurman, *Sermons on the Parables*, ed. David B. Gowler and Kipton Jensen (Maryknoll, NY: Orbis Books, 2018), 31.

11. Noted by Harvey, *Thurman*, 12. Saul Thurman, who died when Thurman was seven, was not his biological father: Peter Eisenstadt, *Against the Hounds of Hell: A Life of Howard Thurman* (Charlottesville: University of Virginia Press, 2021), 33. Thurman was raised by his mother and grandmother and did not have a male sibling.

12. Sermon "Footprints of the Disinherited," May 31, 1972, *PHWT* 5:228–29. The not "condemned forever" to do their master's will is included in Howard Thurman, *The Luminous Darkness* (Richmond, IN: Friends United Press, 1989), 101.

13. Thurman, "Footprints of the Disinherited," *PHWT* 5:230. Thurman notes here that for the disinherited, "love is something that initially is practiced in the tiny cell in which, in their society, they have been imprisoned," but that the practice

of love, as Pentecost demonstrates, must "broaden the magnetic field of [their] Christian morality to include...[people] who are not [them]."

14. Thurman, *Sermons*, 29. Thurman's focus on "What Is God Like?" is likely influenced by his reading of George Buttrick, *The Parables of Jesus* (New York: Richard R. Smith, 1930), 176–86.

15. Carob pods were usual fodder for animals and the food of desperation for humans who are starving. These "pods" are usually thought to be the pods of an evergreen tree (*Ceratonia siliqua*) which had sweet seeds when ripe.

16. Thurman, *Sermons*, 30.

17. Thurman, "Jesus Speaks of Salvation," HTC: Box 14. Folder 10. Cf. Jonah's failed attempt to flee "from the presence of the LORD" (Jonah 1:3).

18. Luke clearly emphasizes repentance. Although it is ambiguous in the parable itself, a proverb cited by Levine from the rabbinic commentary *Leviticus Rabbah* 13.4 offers an intriguing comparative text possibly linking the son to repentance: "When Israelites are reduced to eating carob pods, they repent"; see Amy-Jill Levine, *Short Stories by Jesus* (New York: HarperOne, 2014), 53. Levine forcefully argues, though, that the son continues to be conniving, not repentant (53–54).

19. Hultgren notes that Luke–Acts uses the noun or verb form of the "conventional" word for repentance twenty-five times (*Parables*, 76) and that nowhere is the term used here a "circumlocution for repentance" (cf. Acts 12:11, where "Peter came to himself," i.e., "realized").

20. Levine, *Short Stories*, 53–54.

21. George Hubbard, *The Teachings of Jesus in Parables* (Boston: Pilgrim Press, 1906), 300–01. David Buttrick puts it more concisely: "I'll go to daddy and sound religious"; see *Speaking Parables* (Louisville, KY: Westminster John Knox Press, 2000), 43. Hubbard believes that the son was moved only after he saw his father's loving reaction, which finally made him understand the nature of his father's love.

22. Cf. similar language in Shepherd of Hermas 1.3.1.

23. For arguments that the son had also angered the community/villagers from his home area, see, for example, Bailey, *The Cross and Prodigal*, 52–55, and Richard Rohrbaugh, "A Dysfunctional

Family and Its Neighbors," in *Jesus and His Parables*, ed. V. George Shillington (Edinburgh: T&T Clark, 1997), 141–64.

24. Michal Beth Dinkler, "'The Thoughts of Many Hearts Shall Be Revealed': Listening in on Lukan Interior Monologues," *Journal of Biblical Literature* 133, no. 2 (2015): 382.

25. Archimandrite Vasileios, *The Parable of the Prodigal Son* (Montreal: Alexander Press, 1999), 15, quoting the Service of the Holy Unction, Fifth Prayer, in the *Service Book of the Holy Orthodox-Catholic Apostolic Church.*

26. "Jesus Speaks of Salvation," HTC: Box 14, Folder 10.

27. "Jesus Speaks of Salvation," HTC: Box 14, Folder 10, 2–3.

28. "Jesus Speaks of Salvation," HTC: Box 14, Folder 10, 5–6.

29. "Jesus Speaks of Salvation," HTC: Box 14, Folder 10, 7.

30. See Howard Thurman's appropriately titled *The Inward Journey* (Richmond, IN: Friends United Press, 1971).

31. Howard Thurman, *WHAH*, 114–15, 120.

32. Howard Thurman, *The Creative Encounter* (Richmond, IN: Friends United Press, 1972), 23–24.

33. Thurman, *Sermons*, chapter 3, "The Prodigal Son." I emphasize *is* in my transcription of the sermon because of how I hear Thurman's own emphasis in the recording.

34. *PHWT* 4:99. Sermon, 1955: "Limitation of Intake."

35. *PHWT* 4:103. Sermon, 1955: "Limitation of Intake."

36. Thurman, *Sermons*, 117–18.

37. Thurman, *Sermons*, 122.

38. Eisenstadt notes that in the mid-1920s, the Genesee River (not the Erie Canal) flowed under some of downtown Rochester (*Against the Hounds of Hell*, 412).

39. Thurman, *Sermons*, 123.

40. Thurman, *Sermons*, 34.

41. Thurman, *Sermons*, 36.

42. Catherine Cate Coblentz, *The Blue Cat of Castle Town* (New York: David McKay, 1949).

43. See, for example, Howard Thurman's Baccalaureate Address at Spelman College on May 4, 1980, as edited by Jo Moore Stewart, in *The Spelman Messenger* 96, no. 4 (Summer 1980): 14–15. See also, "Sing Your Own Song" in the We Believe Series (March 6, 1964): https://thurman.pitts.emory.edu/items/show/1259.

44. *PHWT* 5:282. "The Sound of the Genuine," May 1, 1977.

45. *PHWT* 5:283–84. "The Sound of the Genuine." See also Thurman, *The Luminous Darkness*, 38.

46. Thurman, *The Luminous Darkness*, 99.

47. This observation *might* have been stimulated by comments in Buttrick, *Parables*, 191.

48. Thurman, *The Creative Encounter*, 39–40.

49. Thurman, *The Creative Encounter*, 34, 37–38.

50. Howard Thurman, *Disciplines of the Spirit* (Richmond, IN: Friends United Press, 1977), 90.

51. Thurman, *Disciplines of the Spirit*, 95.

CHAPTER 6

1. Archimandrite Vasileios, *The Parable of the Prodigal Son* (Montreal: Alexander Press, 1999), 13–14.

2. See David B. Gowler, "The Parable of the Prodigal Son (Luke 15:11–32)," *Bible Odyssey*: https://m.bibleodyssey.org/passages/main-articles/parable-of-the-prodigal-son/.

3. For example, Joel Green argues that there likely are villagers who witness his words and actions toward his son: *The Gospel of Luke* (Grand Rapids: Eerdmans, 1997), 583; and, similarly, Richard Vinson suggests that various townspeople were watching these events: *Luke* (Macon, GA: Smyth & Helwys, 2008), 512.

4. Charles Hedrick, *Many Things in Parables* (Louisville, KY: Westminster John Knox Press, 2004), 40.

5. In addition, Amy-Jill Levine questions other long-held assumptions such as ones popularized by Joachim Jeremias's influential *The Parables of Jesus* (New York: Charles Scribner's Sons, 1962)—his discussion of the Prodigal Son is on pages 128–32. She argues, for example, that the prodigal does not treat his father as if he were dead, the prodigal's problem is hunger not uncleanness (because of feeding swine), it is not surprising that the father is compassionate, and it is not undignified or dishonorable for the father to run to his son. See Amy-Jill Levine, *Short Stories by Jesus* (New York: HarperOne, 2014), 47–57. I do not agree with every detail of Levine's arguments, but her reading is a needed corrective to the sometimes-flawed assumptions of many scholars.

6. See also the comparative texts from the Hebrew Bible, other Jewish writings, and Greco-Roman sources listed in Klyne Snodgrass, *Stories with Intent*, 2nd ed. (Grand Rapids, MI: Eerdmans, 2018), 119–23. Quintilian, for example, writes, "There is a law to the effect that 'the man who refuses to support his parents is liable to imprisonment'" (*Inst.* 5.10.97; cited in Snodgrass, *Stories with Intent*, 121; cf. Lucian, *Abdicatus* 21). The Gospel of Luke itself attests to issues related to inheritance (12:13).

7. Noted in Amy-Jill Levine and Ben Witherington, *The Gospel of Luke* (Cambridge: Cambridge University Press, 2018), 422.

8. David B. Gowler, *Host, Guest, Enemy, and Friend* (Eugene, OR: Wipf & Stock, 2007 [1991]), 256.

9. Howard Thurman, "Jesus Prays" ("The Religion of Jesus #13, March 17, 1957), 2, HTC: Box 12, Folder 8, 158.

10. Howard Thurman, "The Love of God," HTC: Box 11, Folder 132, 130a, 4.

11. Thurman, "The Love of God," 8.

12. Howard Thurman, *Sermons on the Parables*, ed. David B. Gowler and Kipton Jensen (Maryknoll, NY: Orbis Books, 2018), 25.

13. Howard Thurman, "Mysticism and the Experience of Love," HTC: Box 3, Folder 9, 11.

14. Thurman, "Mysticism and the Experience of Love," 13, 16.

15. Thurman, "Mysticism and the Experience of Love," 13–15. Thurman uses as an example the story of the woman accused of adultery in John 8, where Jesus tells her accusers that the one without sin should cast the first stone.

16. Thurman, *Sermons*, 84.

17. Thurman, *Sermons*, 85.

18. Howard Thurman, *Disciplines of the Spirit* (Richmond, IN: Friends United Press, 1977), 121–22.

19. Paul Duke, *The Parables* (Nashville: Abingdon, 2005), 88.

20. Callie Callon, "*Adulescentes* and *Meretrices*: The Correlation between Squandered Patrimony and Prostitutes in the Parable of the Prodigal Son," *Catholic Biblical Quarterly* 75 (2013): 259–78.

21. George Hubbard, *The Teachings of Jesus in Parables* (Boston: Pilgrim Press, 1906), 305.

22. See David B. Gowler, "Sit and Listen; Go and Do: The Parables of the Good Samaritan and Prodigal Son in Howard

Thurman's Life and Thought," in *Anatomies of the Gospels and Beyond the Gospels: Essays in Honor of R. Alan Culpepper*, ed. Elizabeth Struthers Malbon, Mikeal C. Parsons, and Paul N. Anderson (Leiden: E. J. Brill, 2018), 434–451.

23. Thurman, *Sermons on the Parables*, 31–32.

24. Thurman, "The Rich Fool," in *Sermons on the Parables*, 68–69.

25. Howard Thurman, *The Growing Edge* (Richmond, IN: Friends United Press, 1974), 67–68.

26. Paul Harvey, *Howard Thurman & the Disinherited: A Religious Biography* (Grand Rapids, MI: Eerdmans, 2020), 16.

27. *PHWT* 3:297–301, 303. (cf. *The Growing Edge*).

28. *PHWT* 3:297.

29. Henri Nouwen, *The Return of the Prodigal Son* (New York: Doubleday, 1992). The following is similarly argued in Gowler, *WATSA Parables?*, 165–66.

30. "For, indeed, I am the younger son; I am the elder son; and I am on my way to becoming the father": Nouwen, *Prodigal Son*, 23.

31. Nouwen, *Prodigal Son*, 29–38.

32. Nouwen, *Prodigal Son*, 62–88.

33. Nouwen, *Prodigal Son*, 22, 119.

34. Hieromonk Gregorios, *The Parable of the Prodigal Son* (Columbia, MO: Newrome Press, 2013), 3–4; echoing St. Gregory Nyssa and St. Isaac the Syrian.

35. "Love Your Enemy," *PHWT* 3:298–300.

CHAPTER 7

1. Oscar Romero, Twenty-Fifth Sunday in Ordinary Time (Year C), September 18, 1977.

2. Klyne Snodgrass, *Stories with Intent*, 2nd ed. (Grand Rapids, MI: Eerdmans, 2018), 360.

3. Cf. Sam Tsang, *Right Parables, Wrong Perspectives* (Eugene, OR: Wipf & Stock, 2015), 31.

4. Emerson Powery, *The Good Samaritan* (Grand Rapids, MI: Baker Academic, 2022), 25.

5. See Richard Vinson, *Luke* (Macon, GA: Smyth & Helwys, 2008), 304.

6. George Hubbard, *The Teachings of Jesus in Parables* (Boston: Pilgrim Press, 1906), 428–29.

7. See Gowler, *WATSA Parables?*, 69–93.

8. Philip F. Esler, "Jesus and the Reduction of Intergroup Conflict: The Parable of the Good Samaritan in the Light of Social Identity Theory," *Biblical Interpretation* 8 (2000): 337–38; Michael P. Knowles, "What Was the Victim Wearing? Literary, Economic, and Social Contexts for the Parable of the Good Samaritan," *Biblical Interpretation* 12, no. 2 (2004): 155–58.

9. Charles Hedrick, *Parables as Poetic Fictions* (Peabody, MA: Hendrickson, 1994), 105.

10. Amy-Jill Levine, *Short Stories by Jesus* (New York: HarperOne, 2014), 94, who was citing Martin Luther King Jr.'s April 3, 1968, "I've Been to the Mountaintop." See Martin Luther King Jr., *The Radical King*, ed. Cornell West (Boston: Beacon, 2015), 265–75.

11. Both priests and Levites are of the tribe of Levi, but priests were descended from Aaron, the brother of Moses. Levites assisted priests in the temple (e.g., prepared sacrificial animals, were musicians for liturgy, led prayers, etc.).

12. See David B. Gowler, "Sit and Listen; Go and Do: The Parables of the Good Samaritan and Prodigal Son in Howard Thurman's Life and Thought," in *Anatomies of the Gospels and Beyond the Gospels: Essays in Honor of R. Alan Culpepper*, ed. Elizabeth Struthers Malbon, Mikeal C. Parsons, and Paul N. Anderson (Leiden: E. J. Brill, 2018), 434–51.

13. Transcribed from the audio of this broadcast housed in the Special Collections of Emory University's Pitts Theology Library.

14. Howard Thurman, "The Great Incarnate Words," HTC B1.F40.10. Also printed in *Motive* 47 (Jan 1944): 23–26.

15. Howard Thurman, *Meditations of the Heart* (New York: Harper & Brothers, 1953), 46–47.

16. "Mahatma Gandhi," *PHWT* 3:255–62.

17. "Mahatma Gandhi," *PHWT* 3:257–58.

18. "Mahatma Gandhi," *PHWT* 3:260.

19. *PHWT* 2:64–65.

20. "The Significance of Jesus III: Love," *PHWT* 2:65. Thurman's views of socialism developed over the years. He was closer to this view early in his career; after the 1930s such statements were rare.

21. See the discussion in David B. Gowler, *The Parables after Jesus* (Waco, TX: Baylor Academic Press, 2020), 227.

22. *PHWT* 2:65–66.

23. See the brief discussion here: https://parablesreception.blogspot.com/2022/04/the-eye-of-needle-is-not-gate-in.html.

24. This sermon is part of his series on the parables of Jesus that year at the Fellowship Church. My initial thoughts on this issue are found in Gowler, "Sit and Listen; Go and Do," but I am indebted to Powery, *Good Samaritan*, 54–55, for additional insights. Thurman also depicts the lawyer as being sincere. See Howard Thurman, *Sermons on the Parables*, ed. David B. Gowler and Kipton Jensen (Maryknoll, NY: Orbis Books, 2018), 49–51.

25. Thurman, *Sermons on the Parables*, 49–51.

CHAPTER 8

1. Texts that have the triad of priest, Levite, and Israelite include the Mishnah (e.g., m. Gittin 5:8). See also Ezra 10:5; Nehemiah 11:3.

2. See Klyne Snodgrass, *Stories with Intent*, 2nd ed. (Grand Rapids, MI: Eerdmans, 2018), 345–47.

3. See F. Scott Spencer, "2 Chronicles 28:5–15 and the Parable of the Good Samaritan," *Westminster Theological Journal* 46 (1984): 317–49. Cf. John Drury, *Parables in the Gospels* (London: Crossroad, 1985), 134–35; Amy-Jill Levine, *Short Stories by Jesus* (New York: HarperOne, 2014), 102–3.

4. Michael P. Knowles, "What Was the Victim Wearing? Literary, Economic, and Social Contexts for the Parable of the Good Samaritan," *Biblical Interpretation* 12, no. 2 (2004): 148–49.

5. Emerson Powery, *The Good Samaritan* (Grand Rapids, MI: Baker Academic, 2022), 93. He also notes (cf. Thurman in the next section) that "compassion" is usually associated with an "empathy" that includes the desire to assist another person, whereas "pity" can be associated with negative feelings or judgments about others (95).

6. Argued convincingly by Douglas Oakman in, for example, "Was Jesus a Peasant? Implications for Reading the Good Samaritan Story," *Biblical Theology Bulletin* 22 (1992): 117–25.

7. Thurman, *JATD*, 79.

8. Thurman, *JATD*, 100–101.

9. Howard Thurman, *Deep Is the Hunger* (New York: Harper & Brothers, 1954), 10–11.

10. Howard Thurman, *Disciplines of the Spirit* (Richmond, IN: Friends United Press, 1977), 114–15.

11. Howard Thurman, "Memories Crowd upon Us," in *Meditations of the Heart* (New York: Harper & Brothers, 1953), 43.

12. As noted by Peter Eisenstadt in private correspondence, Thurman observes that pity can be a manifestation of white supremacy, where it serves as a way of distancing and othering African Americans. As Thurman also wrote, "*If a man can feel sorry for you, he can very easily absolve himself from dealing with you in any sense as an equal*": Howard Thurman, *Footprints of a Dream: The Story of the Church for the Fellowship of All Peoples* (Eugene, OR: Wipf and Stock, 2009), 47 (italics in the original).

13. Thurman, "Not Pity, but Compassion," in *Meditations of the Heart*, 49.

14. Howard Thurman, *Deep River and The Negro Spiritual Speaks of Life and Death* (Richmond, IN: Friends United Press, 1975), 95.

15. Thurman, "Enthusiasm and Self-Sacrifice" in *Meditations of the Heart*, 80–81.

16. "The Significance of Jesus VI": *PHWT* 2:85. That reverence extends also to both fauna and flora (85). Cf. Thurman's 1937 lecture "Man and the World of Nature" (*PHWT* 2:103–6), which is an extended discussion of environmentalism as a religious response.

17. "The Significance of Jesus VI": *PHWT* 2:88.

18. "The Significance of Jesus VI": *PHWT* 2:89–90.

19. *PHWT* 1:36–41.

20. Paul Harvey, *Howard Thurman & the Disinherited: A Religious Biography* (Grand Rapids, MI: Eerdmans, 2020), 40–41.

21. Howard Thurman, *Sermons on the Parables*, ed. David B. Gowler and Kipton Jensen (Maryknoll, NY: Orbis Books, 2018), 47–56.

22. George Buttrick, *Parables of Jesus* (New York: Richard R. Smith, 1930), 152–54.

23. Buttrick, *Parables of Jesus*, 153–54.

24. Thurman, *Sermons on the Parables*, 51.

25. Thurman, *Sermons on the Parables*, 56.

26. HTC Box 12, Folder 1, 151.a–c.

27. Luther E. Smith Jr., *Howard Thurman: The Mystic as Prophet*, 3rd ed. (Richmond, IN: Friends United Press, 2007), 17, 34.

28. Thurman, *Sermons on the Parables*, 140–41.

29. Thurman, *Sermons on the Parables*, 56.

CHAPTER 9

1. Thurman, "The Perils of Preaching the Love Ethic of Jesus," HTC Box 6, Folder 6.

2. Bruce W. Longenecker, "The Story of the Samaritan and the Innkeeper (Luke 10:30–35): A Study in Character Rehabilitation," *Biblical Interpretation* 17 (2009): 423.

3. The parable in Matthew 20:1–16 indicates that a denarius was a day's wage for the laborers in the vineyard.

4. Charles Hedrick, *Parables as Poetic Fictions* (Peabody, MA: Hendrickson, 1994), 112–13.

5. Walter Wink, "The Parable of the Compassionate Samaritan," *Review and Expositor* 76, no. 2 (1979): 211.

6. Part of the following stems from David B. Gowler, "'You Shall Love the Alien as Yourself': Hope, Hospitality, and Love of the Stranger in the Teachings of Jesus," *Religions* 10, no. 3 (2019): 220.

7. E.g., longer-term "strangers," such as resident aliens, who were offered protection and provided for in Jewish law. Cf. Andrew Arterbury, *Entertaining Angels* (Sheffield: Sheffield Phoenix Press, 2005), 131–32; Christine D. Pohl, *Making Room: Recovering Hospitality as a Christian Tradition* (Grand Rapids, MI: Eerdmans, 1999), 3–15.

8. Deanna Thompson, *Deuteronomy* (Louisville, KY: Westminster John Knox Press, 2014), 14.

9. Joel Green, *The Gospel of Luke* (Grand Rapids, MI: Eerdmans, 1997), 426.

10. Ruben Zimmermann, *Puzzling the Parables* (Minneapolis: Fortress, 2015), 313.

11. Howard Thurman, "The Desert Dweller," in Howard Thurman, *Meditations of the Heart* (New York: Harper & Brothers, 1953), 90–91.

12. Thurman, *Meditations of the Heart*, 90–91.

13. Longenecker, "The Samaritan and the Innkeeper," 440.

14. Emerson Powery, *The Good Samaritan* (Grand Rapids, MI: Baker Academic, 2022), 26.

15. Longenecker, "The Samaritan and the Innkeeper," 444–45. Cf. Powery, who discusses how Martin Luther King Jr.'s famous sermon at Riverside Church in New York City on April 4, 1967 (discussed in chapter 7), extends the parable to address unjust structural systems and how John Lewis exemplified such "good trouble" of advocating for civil rights and legislation (*Good Samaritan*, 143–45).

16. Thurman, *Meditations of the Heart*, 111–12.

17. Thurman, *Meditations of the Heart*, 112.

18. Howard Thurman, "Mysticism and the Experience of Love," HTC Box 3, Folder 9, 18. A version of this idea is also found in "In His Image," in Howard Thurman, *The Inward Journey* (Richmond, IN: Friends United Press, 1971), 120–21.

19. Thurman, "For Meditation," HTC Box 10, Folder 16, k.

20. HTC Box 3, Folder 9, 20–21, 23.

21. HTC Box 3, Folder 9, 19.

22. William Blake, *The Complete Prose and Poetry of William Blake*, ed. David V. Erdman (Berkeley: University of California Press, 1982), 205.

23. HTC Box 13, Folder 54, 312.

24. Thurman, "Mysticism and Social Action," HTC Box 8, Folder 35, 35.

25. David E. Garland, *Luke* (Grand Rapids, MI: Zondervan, 2011), 446.

26. Howard Thurman, *Sermons on the Parables*, ed. David B. Gowler and Kipton Jensen (Maryknoll, NY: Orbis Books, 2018), 127–28.

27. Thurman, *Sermons on the Parables*, 128, 130–31.

28. Howard Thurman, *Deep Is the Hunger* (New York: Harper & Brothers, 1951), xi.

29. See Thurman's 1946 sermon, "Apostles of Sensitiveness": *PHWT* 3:170–74.

30. Barbara Brown Taylor, "Eccentric Apostles Leading from the Growing Edge," in *The Unfinished Search for Common Ground*, ed. Walter E. Fluker (Maryknoll, NY: Orbis Books, 2023), 70.

31. "Apostles of Sensitiveness," *PHWT* 3:171–72.

32. Howard Thurman, *The Luminous Darkness* (Richmond, IN: Friends United Press, 1989), 61; Thurman, *WHAH*, 195.

33. Noted and cited in *PHWT* 3:xxxv.

34. Thurman, "Mysticism and Social Change," *PHWT* 2:214.

35. Thurman, "Mysticism and Social Change," *PHWT* 2:215. "Narrow" interests can include self-gratification or some type of reward from God.

36. Thurman cites such examples as having "possession of the means of production" that gives people (greater) control over their own interests; "Mysticism and Social Change," *PHWT* 2:216.

37. Thurman, "Mysticism and Social Change," 217–18.

38. "The Significance of Jesus II: The Temptations of Jesus," September 13, 1937: *PHWT* 2:58. See also Thurman, *The Luminous Darkness*, 12–14.

39. HTC Box 6, Folder 6.

40. HTC Box 6, Folder 6, 2–3.

41. HTC Box 6, Folder 6, 8.

42. HTC Box 6, Folder 6, 8.

43. Dmitri Royster, *The Parables* (Crestwood, NY: St. Vladimir's Seminary Press, 1966), 119.

44. Mikeal Parsons, *Luke: Storyteller, Interpreter, Evangelist* (Peabody, MA: Hendrickson, 2007), 181.

45. Noted by Zimmermann, *Puzzling the Parables*, 320.

46. Sylvia Keesmaat, "Strange Neighbors and Risky Care," in *The Challenge of Jesus' Parables*, ed. Richard Longenecker (Grand Rapids, MI: Eerdmans, 2000), 283–84.

47. George Buttrick, *Parables of Jesus* (New York: Richard R. Smith, 1930), 151.

48. Buttrick, *Parables*, 153.

49. Zimmermann, *Puzzling the Parables*, 322–23.

50. Hedrick, *Parables as Poetic Fictions*, 113.

51. Cf. Garland, *Luke*, 436.

52. Noted by Bernard Brandon Scott, *Hear Then the Parable: A Commentary on the Parables of Jesus* (Minneapolis: Fortress Press, 1989), 190.

CHAPTER 10

1. Muriel Rukeyser, "Islands." Used by permission of William L. Rukeyser.

2. As the proud father of two sons, I am delighted to say that this story is about our sons, Camden and Jacob, who have proven over the many years since this event occurred that they truly are connected.

3. Howard Thurman, *WHAH*, 239–40.

4. HTC Box 82, Folder 30, 179. See also the "Peter the Penguin" short story and "Paddy the Penguin," in HTC Box 16, Folder 49, Q.

5. Luther Smith, *Howard Thurman: The Mystic as Prophet*, 3rd ed. (Richmond, IN: Friends United Press, 2007 [1991]), 212.

6. HTC Box 11, Folder 66.

7. "The Religion of Jesus and Social Change II," HTC Box 11, Folder 67.

8. Howard Thurman, *The Luminous Darkness* (Richmond, IN: Friends United Press, 1989), 112–13. Cf. Howard Thurman, *The Search for Common Ground* (Richmond, IN: Friends United Press, 1986), 6.

9. Thurman, *The Luminous Darkness*, 98–99.

10. Howard Thurman, *Meditations of the Heart* (New York: Harper & Brothers, 1953), 104–5. Naylor (or Nayler) sonnets, first published in 1945, were written by Kenneth Boulding and based on the last words of James Naylor (or Nayler, as he is more often called), an early member of the Society of Friends (Quakers) who died in 1660.

11. Thurman, *Meditations of the Heart*, 105.

12. Howard Thurman, *The Inward Journey* (Richmond, IN: Friends United Press, 1971), 106.

13. Thurman, *Meditations of the Heart*, 116.

14. Thurman, *Meditations of the Heart*, 114–17.

15. Thurman, *Meditations of the Heart*, 120–21.

16. Thurman, *Meditations of the Heart*, 121–23.

17. Thurman, *Meditations of the Heart*, 168–71. Compare Abraham Lincoln's early address (1842) to the temperance society of Springfield, IL. As Jon Meacham writes, "To be hectored and condemned; to be told that they were wholly wrong" was for Lincoln "a path not to reform but to intransigence." "If you would win a man to your cause," he quotes Lincoln, "*first* convince him that you are his sincere friend." https://www.washingtonpost.com/

opinions/2022/10/25/abraham-lincoln-jon-meacham-biography-polarized-politics/.

18. Cited by Philip Esler, "Jesus and the Reduction of Intergroup Conflict: The Parable of the Good Samaritan in the Light of the Social Identity Theory," *Biblical Interpretation* 8 (2000): 348.

19. The original essay can be found in Adam Serwer, *The Cruelty Is the Point* (New York: One World, 2021), 100–105.

20. Thurman, *The Luminous Darkness*, 38–39, 44–45.

21. See the discussion in chapter 9. Cf. Howard Thurman, *Deep Is the Hunger* (New York: Harper & Brothers, 1951), 108–9.

22. Using the example found in "Footprints of the Disinherited," *PHWT* 5:228–29 (with selections from *PHWT* 5:225–32 and the draft in HTC Box 6, Folder 50).

23. *PHWT* 5:230.

24. Howard Thurman, *Deep River and The Negro Spiritual Speaks of Life and Death* (Richmond, IN: Friends United Press, 1975), 59–60.

25. Smith, *Mystic as Prophet*, 128.

26. Thurman, "Mysticism and Social Action," HTC Box 8, Folder 39.

27. Thurman's working definition of *mysticism* in this lecture is "the response of the individual to a personal encounter with God within his own soul": HTC Box 8, Folder 39, 18.

28. HTC Box 8, Folder 39, 19.

29. HTC Box 8, Folder 39, 21. Emphasis mine.

30. Smith, *Mystic as Prophet*, 148.

31. First stated by Theodore Parker and often quoted by Martin Luther King Jr.

32. Peter Eisenstadt, *Against the Hounds of Hell: A Life of Howard Thurman* (Charlottesville: University of Virginia Press, 2021), 177; Reinhold Niebuhr, *Moral Man and Immoral Society* (New York: Charles Scribner's, 1932), xvii.

33. Smith, *Mystic as Prophet*, 214. See also, Walter Fluker, "Creating and Cultivating Democratic Spaces," in *The Unfinished Search for Common Ground* (Maryknoll, NY: Orbis Books, 2023), 199–220.

34. Thurman's perspective is a precursor to both liberation theology and Black theology, but serious questions, for example, can be raised about what types of "shocks to the system" are necessary

to bring about justice, equality, and positive social change (see Smith, *Mystic as Prophet*, 158–59, 207).

35. *PHWT* 2:xxi, xxiv.

36. *PHWT* 5:212.

37. *PHWT* 5:312, 317.

38. *PHWT* 5:317.

CHAPTER 11

1. The maxim used by Senator Paul Wellstone to illustrate his core belief, probably first used in a 1999 speech to the Sheet Metal Workers Union.

2. The Dalai Lama, https://twitter.com/DalaiLama/status/1619999014627459072.

3. See Carol Anderson, *White Rage: The Unspoken Truth of Our Racial Divide* (New York: Bloomsbury, 2016).

4. Luther Smith, "Prophetic Vision and Its Radical Consequences," in *The Unfinished Search for Common Ground*, ed. Walter Fluker (Maryknoll, NY: Orbis Books, 2023), 29.

5. Howard Thurman, *Disciplines of the Spirit* (Richmond, IN: Friends United Press, 1977), 122.

6. Howard Thurman, "The Significance of Jesus VI," *PHWT* 2:89; Walter Fluker in *The Unfinished Search for Common Ground*, 11; Smith, "Prophetic Vision," 27.

7. Lobsang Tenzin Negi, "Apostles of Sensitiveness," in Fluker, *The Unfinished Search for Common Ground*, 112–23.

8. Negi, "Apostles of Sensitiveness," 113. See also, His Holiness the Dalai Lama, *Beyond Religion: Ethics for a Whole World* (New York: Houghton Mifflin Harcourt, 2011).

9. Negi, "Apostles of Sensitiveness," 116, 118–21.

10. See Thurman's sermon "Buddha," in *The Way of the Mystics* (Maryknoll, NY: Oribis Books, 2021), 25–33.

11. De Waal quotes Charles Darwin, who stated in *The Descent of Man*, "Any animal whatever, endowed with well-marked social instincts...would inevitably acquire a moral sense or conscience, as soon as its intellectual powers had become as well developed...as in man." De Waal also cites the parable of the Good Samaritan in his *New York Times*, October 17, 2010, "Opinionator" column. Cf. its use in de Waal, *The Age of Empathy:*

Nature's Lessons for a Kinder Society (New York: Crown, 2009), 89–90, where seminarians sent to preach on the parable fail to live up to its message.

12. For example, the work of Meredith Crawford (1937) at the Yerkes Center, where chimpanzees learned to cooperate, and that cooperation extends to help another chimpanzee, even when others do not benefit (because of past or future reciprocity). See de Waal, *The Age of Empathy*, 118–57.

13. See Jamil Zaki, *The War for Kindness: Building Empathy in a Fractured World* (New York: Broadway Books, 2020), especially 267.

14. See the discussion in chapter 2 (cf. *PHWT* 5:155–56).

15. Jamil Zaki, *The War for Kindness*, 47–49.

16. Peter Blake, "Evolving the Ingredients for Reciprocity and Spite," in *Philosophical Transactions of the Royal Society B* 364 (2009): 3255–66.

17. *PHWT* 5:227.

18. Heather McGhee, *The Sum of Us: What Racism Costs Everyone and How We Can Prosper Together* (New York: One World, 2021), xxi, 6, 14. For example, the predatory subprime loans that helped precipitate the 2008 financial crisis initially (in the 1990s) were focused on Black and brown families. Once lenders discovered how profitable such predatory loans were, adjustable rate mortgages (ARMs) were created for a broader market (93). This greed became a financial disaster for many.

19. I was saddened to learn that St. Louis similarly closed the largest swimming pool in the United States, the Fairground Park pool, in the mid-1950s, two miles from where my maternal grandparents had lived in the early 1940s (McGhee, *The Sum of Us*, 26–27). For more details about the history of such racial injustices in St. Louis, see Walter Johnson, *The Broken Heart of America* (New York: Basic Books, 2020), esp. 261–64.

20. McGhee, *The Sum of Us*, 28.

21. McGhee, *The Sum of Us*, 45, 48.

22. McGhee, *The Sum of Us*, 38, 56.

23. McGhee, *The Sum of Us*, 86, 97.

24. See Howard Thurman, "The Rich Fool," in *Sermons on the Parables*, ed. David B. Gowler and Kipton E. Jensen (Maryknoll, NY: Orbis Books, 2018), 74–75, in which he describes how the wealthy attempt to use their wealth to protect themselves from the vicissitudes in life but in the end erect barriers that harm

their relationships with others and with God. Cf. the examples in McGhee, *The Sum of Us*, 202–3.

25. McGhee, *The Sum of Us*, 21, 63.

26. McGhee, *The Sum of Us*, 181, 281.

27. *PHWT* 4:2.

28. *PHWT* 4:7–8. Thurman uses the parable of the Talents (Matt 25:14–30) in a 1950 address at Howard University School of Religion to warn that it is our *job to work at it* and to trust God beyond that point (*PHWT* 4:28–29).

29. Amy-Jill Levine, *Short Stories by Jesus* (New York: HarperOne, 2014), 69.

30. Other studies correlate with and extend these results (e.g., students who forgive perform better academically). See Tara Parker-Pope, "Why You Should Practice Forgiveness," *Washington Post*, April 27, 2023, https://www.washingtonpost.com/wellness/2023/04/27/forgiveness-practice/. See also the Human Flourishing Program at Harvard's Institute for Quantitative Social Science, https://hfh.fas.harvard.edu/. The REACH model for forgiveness by Everett Worthington may be found here: https://www.evworthington-forgiveness.com/reach-forgiveness-of-others.

31. I accessed the 2023 report here: World Happiness Report, "World Happiness Report 2023," https://worldhappiness.report/ed/2023/.

32. See the entry under chapter 4 here: https://worldhappiness.report/ed/2023/executive-summary/. See also the discussion about how Thurman cited similar experiments about kindness, ranging from how mice responded positively to kindness to how human beings did: *Disciplines of the Spirit*, 106–8.

33. Howard Thurman, "The Religion of Jesus: Poverty and Riches," January 27, 1957: HTC Box 12, Folder 3, 153, 4.

34. Christopher Marshall, *Compassionate Justice* (Eugene, OR: Cascade Books, 2012).

35. Gowler, *WATSA Parables?*, 172–74.

36. Walter Mosley, *Blue Light* (New York: Little, Brown, and Co., 1998), 277.

37. Howard Thurman, "The Love of God," in Howard Thurman, *The Growing Edge* (Richmond, IN: Friends United Press, 1974), 67.

38. Howard Thurman, *The Creative Encounter* (Richmond, IN: Friends United Press, 1972), 121–22.

39. Thurman, "The Love of God," 68.

40. Sylvia Keesmaat, "Strange Neighbors and Risky Care," in *The Challenge of Jesus' Parables*, ed. Richard Longenecker (Grand Rapids, MI: Eerdmans, 2000), 265.